MARATHON
THE WORLD OF THE LONG-DISTANCE ATHLETE

MARATHON
THE WORLD OF THE
LONG-DISTANCE ATHLETE

Gail Campbell

STERLING PUBLISHING CO., INC. NEW YORK

Oak Tree Press Co., Ltd.
London & Sydney

OTHER BOOKS OF INTEREST

Bike-Ways
Body-Building and Self-Defense
Competing in Cross-Country Skiing

Easy Motorcycle Riding
Exercise for Sports
Guinness Sports Record Book

Olympic Gymnastics
Skiing on the Level
Successful Track & Field

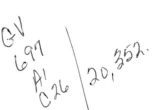
Dedicated with love
To Jim, my other half and fellow marathoner. May we be as healthy, happy, and crazy during our second decade together as we have been during the first . . .
To Andy, Mike, and Phil for their invaluable support, advice, and general lunacy . . .
And to the West Valley Joggers and Striders for sharing their joy of running for fun and competition.

ACKNOWLEDGMENTS

The author and publishers wish to thank the following for the photographs they supplied for this book: Associated Press, London; Harmsworth Photo Library; E. D. Lacey; Planet News Ltd.; Radio Times; United Press International, Inc.; and especially Wide World Photos.

Copyright © 1977 by Gail Campbell
Published 1977 by Sterling Publishing Co., Inc.
Two Park Avenue, New York, N.Y. 10016
Distributed in Australia and New Zealand by Oak Tree Press Co., Ltd.,
P.O. Box J34, Brickfield Hill, Sydney 2000, N.S.W.
Distributed in the United Kingdom and elsewhere in the British Commonwealth
by Ward Lock Ltd., 116 Baker Street, London W 1
Manufactured in the United States of America
All rights reserved
Library of Congress Catalog Card No.: 76-5862-5
Sterling ISBN 0-8069-4114-6 Trade   Oak Tree 7061-2551-7
4115-4 Library

Contents

The First Marathon

In 490 B.C., a fully armed courier ran from the battlefield on the Plains of Marathon to Athens to announce that the heavily outnumbered Greek army had repulsed a Persian invasion. The unknown Greek covered 24 strenuous miles and had barely gasped, "Rejoice! We've won," when he collapsed and fell dead.

The prelude to the Battle of Marathon was even more dramatic. When the Athenians learned that the Persians were on their way to conquer and enslave Greece, the champion Greek runner, Pheidippides, was sent to solicit the aid of the Spartans. He ran for two days and two nights, swimming rivers, crossing mountains, and eventually totaling 158 miles. Pheidippides negotiated with the Spartans for

a full day and immediately returned home with the news that the Spartans would help as soon as their religious festival ended. His astounding run covered over 300 miles of rough terrain in only four days. The Athenians repaid him by building a temple in his honor.

In 1896, the marathon was introduced into the modern Olympic Games in Athens and was run over the original 24-mile course. During the 1908 Olympics in London, the distance was increased as a favor to King Edward VII and Queen Alexandra. The race began on the lawns of Windsor Castle and finished at White City Stadium, 26 miles 385 yards away. This then became the official distance for all marathons and remains so today.

I. THE DISTANCE RUNNER

Abebe Bikila

1. Marathon Motivation

Marathon runners seem to be either blessed —or burdened—with a fierce determination which drives them beyond the normal limits of human endurance. This is revealed in the story of Felix Carvajal, a Cuban postman from Havana.

In 1904, Felix heard that the Olympic Games that year were to be held in conjunction with the World's Fair in St. Louis, Missouri. He had always dreamed of winning the Olympic marathon even though he had never run a competitive race in his life nor the then marathon distance of 24 miles. In spite of his lack of experience, he was determined to run in the 1904 race.

Felix's main problem was lack of money to pay for the trip from Havana to St. Louis. Not being deterred by this in the least, he quickly came up with a plan to run in the public square in Havana to attract attention to his cause. He begged for contributions to send him to the Olympics, and by summer had enough money to sail to America.

Unfortunately, Felix's first stop was New Orleans where he lost all his hard-earned money to gamblers. His unfaltering determination, however, led him through this crisis. The Olympic Games were to start soon, so he set out on foot, running from New Orleans to St. Louis, 700 miles away. Since he was racing against time as well as distance, he had little rest or sleep during the arduous trip.

Felix finally reached the site of the games on August 30th but had only a few hours until the beginning of the marathon. When he approached the starting line, his fellow runners laughed in disbelief at his appearance. He was dressed in a long-sleeved shirt, long pants, and heavy walking shoes. A compassionate bystander with a pair of scissors cut his pant legs off at the knee.

The day was broiling hot and took a heavy toll from the 30 starting runners. By the half-way point, the scorching heat, thick suffocating dust from the roads, and sheer physical exhaustion forced many to collapse or quit. Felix astounded everyone with his endurance as he plodded along. When it was finally over, 14 runners had completed the grueling race and Felix placed a very respectable fourth. Felix Carvajal may be remembered in history as the most magnificent loser of the Olympic marathon.

The question most commonly asked of athletes who compete in marathon sports is "Why?" To the uninitiated it seems masochistic and pointless to run $26\frac{1}{4}$ miles, swim the turbulent English Channel, or pedal a bike over mountains and valleys for 3,000 miles. It is incomprehensible that men, women, and even children suffer cramps, injuries, and sometimes death to compete for merely a wreath, trophy, or place in a record book. Even Frank Shorter, the winner of the 1972 Olympic marathon (see page 51), has admitted that a successful distance runner cannot be goal-oriented. There must be something greater than winning that drives these great athletes on.

The reasons given for competing in marathons are varied and often vague. Some people seek the recognition, however slight, that they

King Edward VII of England is here shown opening the Olympic Games on July 13, 1908, in London at the time that the official marathon distance of 26 miles 385 yards was established.

can find through competition. A very small percentage enter endurance sports to earn a living. The most common motivation, however, is the physical and psychological sense of well-being it brings. Many individuals have found that the best way to combat the nervous tension and anxiety of today's fast-paced world is through intense exercise. A number of champion distance swimmers and runners have become successful while undergoing great emotional stresses caused by divorce, financial problems, and so on. This may be in part because they turned to training which acted as a powerful tranquilizer for them.

Although such endurance feats are found almost exclusively in sports today, they were once necessary for man's survival. Eskimos and African hunters stayed on the move for days while tracking prey. The Tarahumara Indians of Mexico relentlessly pursued deer on foot until the animal dropped dead from exhaustion. Even today this tribe which calls itself *Rarámuri*, or "foot runners," still shuns horses and burros while traveling through the mountains and canyons of their homeland.

The Tarahumaras are also known for their running game, *rarajípari*, a sort of marathon kickball. In this game, two teams of men run barefoot for 6 to 48 hours, often covering over 100 miles, while kicking a lightweight wooden ball. At night, torches light their way while rattles on their belts keep them awake. Nourished only with corn gruel or water, they cross the finish, barely breathing hard but occasionally suffering from slight leg cramps.

Two of these tribesmen once entered the $26\frac{1}{4}$-mile Olympic marathon but lost first place by a few minutes. Aurelio Terrazas and José Torres seemed shocked when someone stopped them past the finish line to say that the race was over. Apparently, they were unaware of where the line was for they protested, "Too short! Too short!"

Running has also been an integral part of the lives of the Himalayan letter-carriers. In carrying mail from their mountain-climbing neighbors to civilization, these runners travel over 100 miles in less than 24 hours.

At the turn of the century, Alaskan pioneers employed professional packers to carry food, clothing, and equipment on packboards. Apparently, these men could carry up to 120 pounds through the mountainous wilderness and were more efficient than pack animals. The Sherpas in the Himalayas still perform such feats—at altitudes of 10,000 to 20,000 feet!

Endurance sports have been popular for centuries in all parts of the world. In England during the 1700's and 1800's, amateur and professional race-walks were a favorite pastime. Thousands of dollars in bets were placed on races in which men averaged 50 to 90 miles each day traveling on foot between cities.

In America, from the turn of the century up through the Roaring Twenties, marathon athletes were considered heroes. Soon, however, football, baseball, and basketball gained dominance via radio, movies, and eventually television. In addition, as the standard of living in American society improved, people found that they had more time and money to spend on sports. The marathon athlete in time was replaced by the super-hero of today who rarely competes for more than 2 hours at a time.

In spite of the overwhelming predominance

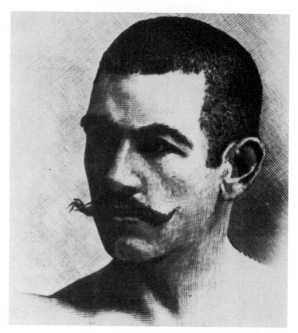

Spyros Louis, winner of the first Olympic marathon, which was introduced into the Games in Athens in 1896. At that time, the distance was 24 miles, representing the original course run by a Greek courier between the Plains of Marathon and Athens in 490 B.C.

of team competition, it is surprising how popular the endurance sports are becoming. The 1976 Boston Marathon, for instance, in the midst of a stifling heat wave, attracted almost 2,000 runners, 70 of whom were women. Hundreds more wanted to compete in this classic race, but the runners had had to qualify in the previous year and be 18 years of age or older.

Some of the better runners today are still in elementary school and junior high. A California youngster, Mary Etta Boitano, completed a $26\frac{1}{4}$-mile marathon at the age of 10 in only 3 hours 1 minute! Apparently, the physiological tools and psychological stamina for marathon competition are a part of our heritage and are available at an early age. Although not a satisfactory answer to the question "Why?" this is the foundation on which each athlete's motivation grows.

2. Fastest on Foot

The fastest marathon runner in history is a 6-foot-2-inch Irish draftsman from Melbourne, Australia, named Derek Clayton. In spite of being unusually tall for a runner, he is the only man ever to complete a marathon course in less than 2 hours 9 minutes. Even though courses differ widely in difficulty, Clayton already has conquered this time barrier twice. On May 30, 1969, in Antwerp he set the present record, 2 hours 8 minutes 33 seconds, by averaging an incredible 4 minutes 54 seconds each mile for over 26 miles.

Clayton is an obsessive, hard-driving runner who believes man is capable of extremely intensive training. Unlike most runners, he logs his daily training mileage at full speed. This extended physical effort can produce bizarre effects. It is not uncommon for such a runner to collapse and become unconscious for 30 to 45 minutes at a time. On one very hot and humid day while finishing a 32-mile training run at top speed, Clayton ran full tilt into a tree. He later admitted that he could see the tree coming but that his legs could not respond fast enough.

As a strong favorite in the 1968 Olympics in Mexico City, Clayton trained harder than ever before. With unfaltering self-discipline, he ran 6 to 7 miles each morning before going to work. In the evenings he logged another 15 to 20 miles clocked at race speeds of 5 to $5\frac{1}{2}$ minutes per mile. To top off these exhausting weekday workouts, each Saturday he sped through the entire distance of a marathon in less than $2\frac{1}{2}$ hours. Clayton's unprecedented training schedule therefore totaled 175 to 220 miles each week, usually at full throttle. This inhuman pace would drive anyone to a physical or mental breakdown. Clayton began dreading his daily workouts and became irritable and uneasy. Before long, these sessions took their toll physically in the form of a cyst on the cartilage of his right knee.

Derek Clayton, fastest marathon runner in history.

11

The Olympics were only two months away, and his leg was stiff, swollen, and extremely painful. Although he needed an operation immediately, Clayton vowed he would run even if it cost him his leg. When he attempted to train, his knee swelled up to the size of a grapefruit. On the day of the Olympics at Mexico City, Clayton shot his leg full of pain killers and entered the race he had prepared for so relentlessly. Clayton pushed himself hard in spite of his handicap and eventually limped across the finish in seventh place only 7 minutes behind first-place winner Mamo Wolde of Ethiopia.

After the Olympics, Clayton returned home to Melbourne and had the long-delayed operation. He began light training sessions again in January and by March was running hard. In May, Clayton miraculously was again breaking world records.

In preparing for the upcoming British marathon championship that year, he altered his training methods by not running as hard as usual. He finished that race only 2 minutes behind the winner, Ron Hill. During the final 10 minutes, however, he was completely dazed and almost unconscious. After he crossed the finish, he moaned that his eyes felt as though they were filled with sand and his stomach filled with writhing snakes. He then fell into a semi-conscious state that lasted for 45 minutes.

The doctor who examined Clayton said that he had over-extended himself. He also ad-

Mamo Walde of Ethiopia winning the 1968 Olympic marathon in Mexico City 7 minutes ahead of Clayton who was running with an agonizingly painful cyst in his knee.

mitted that the runner was basically as strong as a draft horse and would be fit to run another marathon in only 48 hours!

Thus, the fastest marathon runner in history is living proof of his philosophy that man is capable of much more intense training than anyone previously prescribed and that the strength developed from such workouts helps overcome otherwise intolerable pain.

A tense moment is depicted here as 10,000 spectators witness one of the most dramatic events in the history of the marathon. Pietri Dorando, in the lead and just 385 yards short of the finish in the 1908 race, staggered, fell, rose and fell again . . . and again.

3. The Dorando-Hayes Story

The 1908 Olympic marathon not only was famous for establishing a new official course distance, but also for being one of the most dramatic races ever. On July 26, a total of 75 long-distance runners from all over the world gathered in London for the start of the race. Tom Morrissey from Boston was favored to win. Pietri Dorando, a 22-year-old Italian candy-maker, was also a favorite since he had won the Paris Marathon the previous year. Rosy-cheeked Johnny Hayes was entered and, at 17, was the youngest U.S. Olympic team member. Hayes was a department store ribbon clerk who had never run a marathon in his life.

The day of the race was very hot and humid as 100,000 anxious spectators crowded into the stadium to await the finish. The heat took its toll dramatically as one by one the runners fell back to a slower pace or dropped out entirely. The favorite, Tom Morrissey, never was a contender for the lead. A South African, Charles Hefferon, ran a very strong race and led near the finish. With barely 4 miles to go, however, Pietri Dorando inched by Hefferon and took the lead. Soon afterward, the American unknown, Johnny Hayes, also passed Hefferon and swept into second place.

When Dorando entered the stadium, Hayes

was a full 600 yards behind him. With only 385 yards to the finish line, the crowd went wild cheering Dorando on. He reached the track and to the crowd's dismay turned in the wrong direction. The flustered officials quickly lined up trackside forcing him to turn around.

Dorando appeared to be in a trance, however, and faltered. His knees buckled, causing him to stagger and fall. With the finish line in full view only 100 yards away, he agonizingly got up and fell again and again.

Suddenly Johnny Hayes approached, running

The victor of the 1908 Olympic race—little Johnny Hayes, the department store clerk who until then had never run a marathon in his life.

with power and ease. The British officials panicked over this unprecedented crisis and feared for Dorando's life. Dorando's desire to win surged forth from his subconscious, commanding him to get up although his body was spent. The officials rushed onto the track and, lifting the stricken runner up by the arms, half-carried and half-dragged him across the finish line.

Johnny Hayes finished only a few steps behind, looking fresh and strong. As he was being officially proclaimed the winner, Pietri Dorando was placed on a stretcher and carried away. The crowd cried out and objected strongly. After three hours of deliberation, the officials were forced to reverse their decision and announced that Johnny Hayes was the victor. Dorando was disqualified for not completing the race under his own power, and Hefferon was awarded second place.

Pietri Dorando was presented a special gold cup by Queen Alexandra, but Johnny Hayes received the Olympic gold medal. A crowd of nearly one million welcomed home the first American ever to win an Olympic marathon. No other American held that honor until 64 years later in 1972.

Post-race rumors abounded concerning everything from dope involvement to an alleged scheme with P. T. Barnum to commercialize the race. Six months later a rematch between Pietri Dorando and Johnny Hayes was held in New York's old Madison Square Garden. Dorando won that race by 60 yards.

Dorando returned to his candy-making in Italy still insisting that he could have completed the Olympic marathon without assistance. Films of the race, however, reveal a completely exhausted, pitiful figure, totally unaware of his surroundings. Another rumor surfaced stating that he had been gargling Chantilly during the race, and some said that he did indeed appear drunk.

Oddly enough, these dramatic, fictitious-sounding events repeated themselves 46 years later at the British Commonwealth Games in

History repeats itself—46 years after Dorando's collapse in London, the great runner Jim Peters entered the stadium in Vancouver well in front of the field. Suddenly, without warning, he stumbled, fell and never crossed the finish line.

Vancouver, British Columbia. One of the best post-World War II marathon runners was Great Britain's Jim Peters. He was in the lead in the 1954 Vancouver marathon and, as he entered the stadium, he beamed proudly. At that point Peters was several hundred yards ahead of second place. He recalled later that suddenly he felt dizzy and the track appeared to be moving away from him. Panic-stricken, he stumbled, and fell. In a daze he got up and staggered toward what he believed was the finish line. The officials, however, had moved it a few hundred yards away.

The team manager and the trainer, fearing that Peters would seriously hurt himself in his agonizing struggles, ran onto the track and grabbed him. The officials were forced to disqualify him even though he had run a superb 26 miles and had collapsed only a few hundred yards from the finish line.

As a demonstration of their love and respect for the great athlete, Vancouver invited Jim Peters back 13 years later. Wearing his original uniform and waving happily, he completed the lap before 40,000 cheering, misty-eyed fans.

4. The Phantom Finn: Paavo Nurmi

Paavo Nurmi was attracted to running at an early age and ran cross-country at a local boys' club in Turku, Finland. When Paavo was only 12 years old, his father died, plunging his family into poverty and grief. Nurmi was forced to go to work to support his family—six people who now lived cramped together in a one-room dwelling. He worked as an errand boy pushing a cart up and down hills to make his deliveries. This crisis turned Nurmi into a reticent, grave child, but the daily walking built up his legs.

He had always admired great athletes and, in particular, worshipped Hannes Kolehmainen, a champion Finnish runner. When his hero won four races at the 1912 Olympics in Stockholm, Sweden, Nurmi became inspired and started training again. He soon joined an athletic club and developed extreme mental and physical discipline through a Spartan conditioning program. He trained hard to increase his stamina and speed and even ran behind trolley cars to develop an even pace.

Nurmi was inducted into the Army but continued his training with the 1920 Olympic Games in mind. He first gained national attention in the 1919 Army Championships. By 1920, he and Kolehmainen were the best runners in Finland. That year, proudly wearing the Finnish flag on his sky-blue T-shirt, Nurmi made his debut in the Olympics in Antwerp, Belgium.

Holding his body erect and with an even stride, Nurmi ran like a machine. Ignoring his competitors, he ran against his stopwatch.

Paavo lost his first Olympic race, the 5,000 meters (3 miles 188 yards), to a Frenchman, Joseph Guillemot. Later that week, however, he returned to win the 10,000 meters (6 miles 376 yards) and led his team to victory in the 10,000-meter cross-country race. In his first Olympic competition, he had captured two gold medals and one silver.

In preparing for the 1924 Olympics, Nurmi went on to destroy many world record times. He set records in everything from 1,500 meters to 10,000 meters and after four years of this exacting competition, he was ready for the Olympics in Paris.

In the spring of 1924, Nurmi damaged a kneecap. The "Phantom Finn," however, astounded everyone in Paris by attempting what no one had ever tried. On the same afternoon he competed in the Olympic 1,500-meter and 5,000-meter races. In spite of his bad knee he won both races and within 90 minutes had set two new Olympic records.

Two days later he entered the 10,000-meter cross-country race which became known as the "battle in the sun." The broiling heat forced 24 of the 39 starters to collapse and be hospitalized, while Nurmi effortlessly strode up and down hills, over water jumps, and across fields. The amazing Finn won that race and was the only apparently fresh runner to finish.

The following day while his fellow competitors were still in the hospital, Nurmi won and set an Olympic record in the 3,000-meter race. Competing against a most extraordinary field of athletes and undergoing a severe test

When Paavo Nurmi came to the United States in 1925, he entered a special 3-mile event at the Los Angeles Coliseum. Here he is, not only winning, but breaking the record in 14 minutes 15.9 seconds.

of endurance, Nurmi collected four gold medals that year.

In the winter of 1925, Paavo came to the United States to compete in the indoor track circuit. Although he had never raced on board tracks previously, he shattered records with almost every start. In New York in February he became the first runner to complete 2 miles in less than 9 minutes.

In the 1928 Olympic Games in Amsterdam,

17

Holland, Nurmi was considered old for a runner. In spite of this he went on to win the 10,000-meter race and place second in both the 5,000-meter race and the 3,000-meter steeplechase. Paavo ended his Olympic career that year after collecting a total of seven gold medals and three silvers in long-distance races in three Olympic Games.

During that decade this amazing running machine set 13 world records at standard distances from 1 mile to 6 miles and 1,500 meters to 20,000 meters (12 miles 752 yards), in addition to setting innumerable national, Olympic, and indoor records. No other runner has yet won so many championships.

Nurmi's obsessive perfectionism and complete dedication to running were visible in his unique running style. He always appeared stolid and unsmiling, carrying his arms high and striding rhythmically with his long, muscular legs. Although Nurmi's records were eventually broken through better training methods, and so on, he revolutionized long-distance racing tactics, and was the most prolific record-breaker of all time.

Nurmi's career ended on the eve of the 1932 Olympics when officials barred him from the Games on the grounds that he had accepted money for appearing at a meet in Berlin. Even though it was common practice at the time to pay expenses to track and field athletes, Nurmi was singled out and barred from amateur competition for life.

Just twenty years later, in 1952, the public repaid their hero by asking Paavo Nurmi, at 55, to bear the Olympic torch into Helsinki Stadium, Finland, for the inaugural ceremonies. And, during his lifetime, they erected a memorial statue to him at the stadium entrance.

The incomparable Phantom Finn died in 1973, a great distance runner of his time or any time.

The "Phantom Finn" carries the Olympic flame into the stadium at Helsinki during the 1952 opening ceremonies, 20 years after being barred from amateur competition for life.

5. The Bunion Derby

A roar went up from the crowd as the gaunt, emaciated man ran into the ferry building at Weehawken, New Jersey, and stared glassy-eyed at the Manhattan skyline across the Hudson River. Soon a second, sunburned runner swathed in bandages jogged in behind the first. Over the next several hours long hair and beards abounded in the terminal, as a total of 55 sinewy figures limped and hobbled in. These disheveled but unbeaten men formed a unique brotherhood, for together these hardy souls had crossed the mountains and deserts of 13 states, had run and staggered through scorching sunshine, freezing wind, rain, snow, and hail, and finally had completed the 84th and final lap of a 3,422-mile transcontinental marathon.

That day—May 26, 1928—marked the climax of the Roaring Twenties, the unsurpassed age of record-setting when life was lived in superlatives. An unprecedented crowd of 15 million Americans witnessed this astounding foot race which may have attracted greater newspaper coverage than any other sports event in history.

A total of $48,500 in prizes had been offered with the intention of attracting champions worldwide. Instead, the money lured hundreds of freaks and publicity hounds and only a few internationally known runners and former Olympians. What was to be a grueling, dramatic contest, soon turned into a zany carnival of mishaps and blisters.

The idea was conceived by Charles C. ("Cash and Carry") Pyle, the P. T. Barnum of the sports world during the 1920's. Pyle, the son of a Methodist minister, was a man of many talents, having been a boxer, actor, salesman, theatrical manager, and owner of a chain of small-town nickelodeons throughout Illinois. In one way or another he fell back on all of these talents while supervising the notorious "Bunion Derby," as it was soon called.

Pyle's great money-making schemes all started in 1925 when the fast-talking promoter convinced Harold "Red" Grange, the most famous football player in the U.S., to turn professional. Pyle, of course, was to manage Grange. At 44, Cash and Carry, with his mustache, powerful jaw, and silver hair, represented the stereotype of the dapper, smooth-talking entrepreneur. He wore only custom-made clothes, enhanced by a diamond stickpin, derby, spats, and a cane. Using his overwhelming power of persuasion, he easily signed Grange with the Chicago Bears under the conditions that he and Red receive 50 per cent of the gate receipts. Under these terms Pyle and his cohort each made over $100,000 from their 18-game tour of the country. The following year they raked in even more money when Red made a movie. The dollar in 1925 was worth about five times its worth today—and there was no income tax!

In the spring of 1927, Pyle announced to the press that he was organizing a marathon. The

They're off and running in the most astounding foot race in history. Ahead of them lie 3,422 miles of wind, rain, heat, mountains, deserts, torn muscles, calluses, blisters, thirst, hunger, monumental fatigue—and a $25,000 first prize awaiting them in Madison Square Garden. How many of them made it? Fifty-five out of a field of 199.

reporters were uninterested at first, having witnessed everything during that decadent decade from swimming and running to drinking and dancing marathons. However, when Pyle went on to say that this marathon would begin at Los Angeles' Ascot Speedway and end in New York's Madison Square Garden, everyone listened attentively.

The winner was to receive $25,000 of the total $48,500 offered. Upon collecting a $25 entry fee, Pyle promised to finance all feeding and sleeping accommodations for the runners. In addition to entry fees, Pyle was to collect a sum from each town along the route in payment for advertising to be carried in programs on sale for the spectators. Pyle also planned to set up arenas in each stopover where he would charge admission for the townspeople to see the runners. By the day the race was to begin, Pyle had collected over $100,000 from towns along Highway 66 between Los Angeles and Chicago and along the other highways on the route from Chicago to New York City. He also had almost 500 entrants, including top-rated runners, as well as crackpots and publicity seekers.

In February, 1928, the promoter opened a training camp at the Speedway three weeks prior to the race. As the athletes arrived, he had each one sign a contract putting him under his management for the two years following the event. The contract required that each give Pyle 50 per cent of his profits from appearances and movies. Then each runner was given a complete physical, and the 275 competitors who qualified began training. Most of the serious contenders ran 30 to 40 miles each day through the hills of Los Angeles, but even at this early stage many dropped out of the fiasco.

While the runners were preparing for the event, Pyle was determining how he would feed them three times a day as well as bed them down in a strange town each night all the way across the country. In addition, sideshows and other money-making attractions were lined up while programs were being printed.

Pyle arranged for a $25,000 double-decker bus, patriotically named *The America*, to accommodate him and his famous officials (Red Grange, et al) during the three-month excursion. He ordered an only slightly less lavishly decorated van to carry the press. The caravan also included an entire radio broadcasting station, cots, tents, portable showers, and a huge mobile kitchen.

On Sunday, March 4, 1928, a total of 199 starters, grouped according to nationalities, marched onto the muddy Ascot Speedway and then paraded around the track before several thousand paying spectators. At 3:46 p.m., Red Grange exploded the bomb signaling the beginning of the zany event and the mass of runners walked, sprinted, and sprawled in the mud.

Athletes ranged in age from 16 to 63, the oldest being Charles W. Hart who once set a world record for a 100-mile run and who just previously had outrun two horses in England. The motley group of racers included a Hindu philosopher, a boy with one arm, a man with a cane, another in logging boots, and even some of the world's best runners in conventional track suits.

On the first day's grueling run to La Puente, California, Pyle witnessed an unexpected problem which was to plague him throughout the upcoming ordeal. The road to La Puente was lined with hundreds of thousands of non-paying spectators while only a few thousand had paid at the Speedway.

At 5:24 p.m. Hannes Kolehmainen of Finland completed the first day's lap in 1 hour 38 minutes. All of the starters managed to stagger through the first lap and were greeted at La Puente by a comical sideshow featuring a five-legged pig, dancing snakes, and hula-dancing girls. To attract more money-paying spectators, the tired runners awkwardly stood on stage that evening telling jokes or simply saying hello to the audience.

The next morning was typical of what was to come for three months. Up at dawn, grab a quick breakfast, and set off on that day's run trying to arrive at the designated checkpoint by midnight. The winner of the transcontinental event was to be the athlete with the shortest elapsed time between L.A. and New York City.

On the second day of the journey, heavy rains caused painful foot blisters which immediately forced six men from the race. On the third day the clowns and crackpots were separated from the true runners as they attempted to climb the 4,300-foot high Cajon Pass and then run down into the Mojave Desert to Victorville, a distance of 45 miles. Wheezing and coughing through the pass, more than 20 dropped out of the nightmare. Kolehmainen, who had been leading the entire way, suffered a painful torn groin muscle and quit. Two men were hit by cars on the scorching desert road and were left behind, unconscious. Throughout the entire race about 12 runners eventually were run down by cars, motorcycles, and even a wayward bicycle.

When the athletes stumbled into Needles, California, on the eighth day, it was obvious that the first 300 miles of the 3,422-mile race had taken their toll. Only 120 runners arrived, indicating that over one-third had already quit. To make matters worse, only jackrabbits and lizards were witnessing the epic event through the desert, so Pyle was making no income at all. At Needles, the company providing food for the ravenous athletes suddenly raised its prices. When the promoter refused to pay, the cooks simply walked out. After that, the helpless, spent runners were only allowed two 35¢ meals a day and a few sandwiches at small-town cafés along the way.

A Britisher from Southern Rhodesia, Arthur Newton, won lap after lap through the Mojave Desert and again through Arizona. Suddenly near Flagstaff, with a 9-hour lead over the others, Newton severely twisted his ankle and was forced to quit.

At this point a 19-year-old part-Cherokee farm boy from Oklahoma, Andy Payne, took over the lead. He too suffered greatly, however, having contracted tonsillitis. He ran with a fever and a sore, swollen throat. Instead of quitting, Payne merely slowed to a walk, temporarily relinquishing his lead.

In Albuquerque, New Mexico, a severe setback hit the determined caravan. The Chamber of Commerce decided against paying the $5,000 it had promised Pyle for having the runners stop there. Undaunted, Pyle ordered his charges to detour around the city, but to his dismay thousands of unpaying spectators watched anyway. Other towns along the way, realizing that everyone else was reneging, began to ask why they should pay when they too could see the race free.

Meanwhile, the runners, averaging 40 miles per day, entered a blinding snowstorm in Texas. The lead runner pulled a tendon and quit, thus putting Andy Payne back in front. Crossing Oklahoma, his home state, Andy attracted the largest crowds of the entire race, climaxing at one point in around 1,000 cars following him down Highway 66.

Pyle was now facing new problems. The food company that had quit early in the race had now gone to court to collect the $5,000 which Oklahoma City had guaranteed Pyle. The next day even some of the runners went on strike in order to get daily lap prizes. When Pyle refused, they reluctantly re-entered the race anyway.

Payne, having led through his home town of Claremore, Oklahoma, received a warm welcome and celebration there. The Bunion Derby had reached the halfway point after 1,700 miles and 46 days of running. A surprising total of 75 athletes still remained. Pyle was not through with his troubles, however, for his van was barraged with rotten eggs in a small town in Missouri. The villagers were angry that the promoter was planning to stop for the night at a nearby town instead of theirs. Soon afterward, a defunct bank in Champaign, Illinois, confiscated Pyle's luxurious bus, *The America*, claiming that the promoter owed them $21,500. When the court found out, however, that the shrewd promoter was only renting the bus, they immediately returned it to him.

As the entourage struggled onward to Chicago, a few indiscreet runners hitched rides in cars and were subsequently evicted from the race. A much more serious problem arose, however, when another association of towns suddenly reneged on a promise to Pyle of $60,000. In the shadow of this financial disaster, the caravan rolled on anyway since they were already 63 days and 2,400 miles into the ordeal.

As they crossed Indiana, Andy Payne stretched his lead over a New Jersey policeman, John Salo, to 24 hours. From Ohio to New York, 55 dedicated runners continued on without losing a single man. Laps were lengthened to an astounding 75 miles per day which meant that the weary athletes were running 12 to 15 hours daily. They suffered heroically through rain and lightning in Pennsylvania and New York and shin splints in the mountains.

By this time, most of them realized that they had no chance of winning one of the ten cash prizes. Yet their pride drove them onward. While Salo desperately fought to lessen Payne's 14-hour lead, a rumor cropped up that someone was going to put Andy out of the race in Salo's

New Jersey policeman John Salo gave winner Andy Payne a run for his money in the 1928 Bunion Derby, but came in second. Undaunted, he returned the following year to place first in the second — and last — Derby.

hometown, Passaic, New Jersey. No trouble arose, however, as the runners entered the town with a police escort. Later, a paying crowd of 3,000 attended a ceremony honoring their hero.

As the 55 weary runners left Passaic, they entered their 84th and final day of the race. Immense crowds lined the road to Weehawken, New Jersey, where the ferry was to take the athletes to New York City.

The final crushing blow came to the zany marathon when hardly anyone turned out in the big city to greet the runners along 10th Avenue or in Madison Square Garden. Only 3,000 apathetic spectators watched the final 20-mile run in the Garden which had a seating capacity of 15,000. The audience managed to perk up slightly, however, when Andy Payne ran head-on into a concrete pillar only a few laps from the finish. Fortunately, he revived and managed to complete the spectacle and collect his $25,000. His winning time for 3,422 miles was 573 hours 4 minutes 34 seconds.

Of course, rumors abounded that Pyle was broke and could not pay off any of the prize money. He promised that he would have it the following Friday night when all 55 finishers were to run a 26-mile team marathon in the Garden. That night Pyle was true to his word and miraculously awarded the entire $48,500. Salo won the $10,000 second prize, Canadian Philip Granville, who was also a champion walker, collected the $5,000 third prize, and an unemployed Cleveland bartender, Mike Joyce, accepted the $2,500 fourth prize.

Meanwhile, a doctor, having examined Andy Payne after the finish, told him that the pathetic race had knocked 10 years off his life expectancy. Payne used the prize money to pay off the mortgage on his father's farm in Claremore, and permanently retired from running. In 1934, Oklahoma showed its appreciation by electing him to the State Supreme Court.

Pyle had lost about $100,000 on the fiasco. But, to everyone's amazement, rather than crawling back into obscurity, Pyle announced a second annual transcontinental foot race!

This time the race was to be run in the reverse direction, offer $60,000 in prizes, require a $300 entry fee, and athletes were to pay for their own meals and accommodations. Nonetheless, Pyle had more problems than ever in this race, since many Chambers of Commerce throughout the states again reneged on promises, cars were repossessed, Pyle's circus tent in Maryland blew down, and his exotic bus was again lost to creditors.

The majority of the 91 starters in the second transcontinental event had suffered through the first race, and 19 of them finished this one. This Bunion Derby was much more exciting than the previous year's, as the entire race centered around a dramatic contest between John Salo and an Englishman, Peter Gavuzzi.

On the last lap of the incredible event, Salo passed Gavuzzi and won the 3,685-mile, 78-day contest by a mere 3 minutes. In these two Bunion Derbies, the Passaic policeman collected $35,000 in prize money. Ironically, only two years later at a sand-lot baseball game, the indefatigable Salo was hit in the head with a ball and died.

This second transcontinental race wiped Pyle out financially. It took him many years to settle the lawsuits and pay off the total $60,000. But, again the determined, scheming promoter set his mind to work. This time he dreamed up a trans-oceanic dance marathon from New York to the Arch of Triumph in Paris. Fortunately, for him, however, the marathon craze of the Twenties was ending, as the country was plunged into the Great Depression. Pyle could not raise a penny, and the American public was no longer amused by such frivolity.

Cash and Carry Pyle moved to Hollywood, began a thriving radio transcription business, and finally faded into obscurity. In 1939, he was overcome by a heart attack at the age of 57.

6. Barefoot Bikila

One of the foremost marathon runners of recent times is Ethiopia's modern Pheidippides, Abebe Bikila. A member of Emperor Haile Selassie's Imperial Guard, Bikila first attained worldwide recognition in the 1960 Olympics in Rome. In those days he was a thin, reticent 28-year-old soldier who had never previously entered a marathon. Everyone considered him foolish to even attempt it. Not only did Bikila finish that first Olympic race, he ran the fastest marathon ever known at that time, 2 hours 15 minutes 16 seconds. On top of that, Bikila ran the entire 26 miles 385 yards barefooted!

When later asked why he had run barefoot in Rome, he replied that this was not at all unusual for an Ethiopian. He also explained that a runner can get in more steps per minute without shoes. In contradiction to this, Bikila had actually bought track shoes in Rome but had gotten painful blisters from them in training. Therefore, he opted for what was natural to him and his countrymen, running barefoot.

In that same year, Abebe was involved in an attempted coup against his government. The confused palace bodyguards were tricked into thinking that they were protecting the emperor rather than revolting against him. Bikila was told to go home and await further orders. Not long afterward the leaders of the revolt were captured and hanged. Abebe was questioned but apparently was not directly involved in the planning of the uprising.

In 1963, Bikila entered the Boston Marathon and was heavily favored. He led throughout the entire race up to the last five miles when, suddenly afflicted with severe cramps, he was forced to drop back. To everyone's surprise Bikila placed only fifth. His trainer later explained that unlike other runners Abebe had not had any glucose during the race. Without it, lactic acid builds up in the muscles and produces severe cramps.

The next year, 1964, the Olympics were to be held in Tokyo. Misfortune struck Bikila again as he suffered through an appendectomy only four weeks prior to the race. He was determined to recover fast and was back in training only two weeks later. Apparently unhandicapped, Abebe Bikila went on to win in Tokyo in a record-shattering 2 hours 12 minutes 11.2 seconds.

After completing his historic run, Bikila did a series of push-ups and sit-ups amid pandemonium in the stands. Although the spectators thought he was showing off, Abebe explained that this was merely a routine method of avoiding post-race cramps.

The hilly terrain outside Addis Ababa provided an excellent training site for the Olympian. His Ethiopian running companions and teammates were all fellow members of the Palace Guard. After his Tokyo victory, Bikila

Abebe Bikila rounds the halfway mark in the 1964 Olympic marathon in Tokyo, well on his way to a record-shattering win of 2 hours 12 minutes 11.2 seconds.

was appointed sports instructor and training director of the Guard. The greatest and most prized reward of all, however, was his promotion to the rank of first lieutenant despite his lack of officer's training.

Since Ethiopians do not overtly fawn over heroes, this special recognition by the emperor was highly valued by Bikila. Behind the thin, nut-colored face, black mustache, high cheekbones, and Roman nose lies a man of great inner strength and one of the fastest marathon runners in history.

7. The Mania of the Solo Runner

The most famous and most ambitious solo long-distance runner of this century is Australian-born Bill Emmerton. Although not an Olympic marathon runner, Emmerton could probably outclass anyone in endurance and perseverance.

At the age of 49 he gained attention in America by running from Houston, Texas, to Cape Kennedy, Florida, a distance of more than 1,000 miles. In accomplishing this astounding feat, he averaged 40 miles a day.

Emmerton, however, is probably best known for his successful attempts to cross California's torturous Death Valley. In 1968, he tried to find runners to challenge him in the 125-mile run, but no one else would venture to conquer the desert that had taken so many lives.

Bill, therefore, set out alone on a blazing 106°F. (41°C.) day from Shoshone, California, with his wife following in a jeep stocked with first-aid supplies. Only 30 miles from the start, his first crisis arose in the form of a blinding sandstorm. Emmerton was lifted up by the driving winds and sand and was mercilessly bounced for 15 feet. Undaunted, he picked himself up and continued running. After completing a few more miles, he suddenly inhaled noxious sulphur fumes, reeled, and collapsed.

His wife, thinking it was all over, rushed to his side and bathed his temples, massaged his muscles, and drenched his clothes with water. Three minutes later he was up and running as if nothing had happened. Emmerton eventually finished the run with holes cut in his shoes to aid the circulation in his swollen, blistered feet.

Instead of resting on his laurels, Bill decided this run was not long enough. Only four months later he crossed Death Valley again, this time covering 211 miles. The tension was greater than ever prior to this run since six weeks earlier a woman, stranded in the desert, had died of sunstroke after her car had broken down.

The day Bill started the run, the temperature had hit a searing 135°F. (57°C.). He later moaned that this crossing was comparable to running through Hell.

Emmerton always thrived on tests of physical endurance. As a young boy growing up on the rugged Australian island of Tasmania, he worshipped distance cyclists and distance runners. Bill began running seriously at the age of 17. At 25, he became a running insurance man, covering 15-mile routes on foot to collect premiums.

In 1952, Emmerton decided to try to obtain money from his lifelong obsession. He accepted $1,000 to turn professional and bet the money on himself in his first race at 33:1 odds. He lost that race by 2 feet and his second race by only 6 inches.

From 1953 to 1956, Bill won 40 racing titles in distances ranging from 0.5 miles to 60 miles. In addition, he broke the Australian records in both the marathon and the 30-mile race.

Since he was not able to earn enough money

"Comparable to running through Hell," moaned Bill Emmerton after covering 211 miles in sizzling Death Valley, California. Only four months earlier he had made a 125-mile crossing, but came back for more.

through running, Emmerton became a sports broadcaster for an Australian radio station. In addition to this, he continued running about 130 miles each week and, in 1959, made an astounding solo run. Crossing from Launceston to Hobart in Tasmania, Bill covered 100 miles in 20 hours 41 minutes. He eventually ran 125 miles in 26 hours without sleep. He admits that he started dozing off at 3 or 4 a.m., running with his eyes closed for a short time.

In 1962, Emmerton raced against time and weather in ascending Tasmania's highest plateau. Spectators placed bets that he could not do it in less than 48 hours. As he started up from the base, he fought through a heavy downpour which later turned to snow near the summit. Officials following in cars commanded that he give up.

Ignoring their pleas and snatching only 2 hours of rest and no sleep, Emmerton completed his dramatic run of 168½ miles in 42½ hours. One year later he completed two unprecedented runs of 158 miles each in consecutive months. One run was accomplished in only 36 hours. The other traversed Tasmania's "Mountain of Death," Mt. Wellington, where two men previously had died of exposure during a marathon.

A landmark in Emmerton's running career was his marriage to Norma Arkles. While she broadened his interests to include concert-going, he taught her to jog. With Norma's encouragement and assistance, Emmerton became even more inspired. As he traversed the endless miles, she would follow in a jeep, shouting encouragement, and massaging his aching feet when he rested. Norma was warned before their marriage that running was the focal point of Emmerton's life. Being pleasant and adaptable, she adjusted quickly, even accepting Bill's 10-mile run on the morning of their wedding.

A year after his marriage, a brewery paid him to complete a distance run wearing a T-shirt labeled COOPERS STOUT FOR STAMINA. In exchange for running 500 miles across the Australian desert in 100°F. (37.8°C.) heat, Emmerton was paid only $250.

Six months later he was contacted by the International Wool Secretariat. They promised to pay his expenses if he would run the length of Britain (952 miles) dressed in wool shorts. During this solo run Emmerton was near death several times. In some areas of the country he was forced to run carrying an umbrella to deflect sleet and hail.

At one point, demoralized and suffering from blisters and sore muscles, he had to keep telling himself he had only 500 miles to go. He had one scheduled stop in which he was to sprint up a hill and deliver a scroll to the town's mayor. Upon doing this, he started to give a speech to the 4,000 spectators present but suddenly collapsed and passed out for a full five minutes. When he awoke, he jumped to his feet and continued his grueling run. Emmerton completed this solo stunt by running the last 36 hours with only two hours of sleep.

In honor of Montreal's Expo '67, Emmerton announced a 390-mile run from Toronto to Montreal. That run was to be more challenging than he had expected. One morning as he was obliviously plodding down a lonely road in Banff on a 10-mile training run, he stopped dead in his tracks. Only 2 yards in front of him, a huge grizzly bear reared up on his hind legs. Bill instinctively turned and fled for his life, never looking back. Only two days later the newspapers reported that two people were killed by a grizzly bear 250 miles away in Glacier Park.

The most demoralizing part of the Toronto-to-Montreal run occurred near the end, just outside Montreal. A well-intentioned policeman told Emmerton he had only 6 miles to go. He increased his pace significantly thinking he was near the finish, but actually had at least 12 miles remaining. After completing 6 miles and not seeing the end, Emmerton broke down. Totally exhausted, with his nerves shattered, he sobbed uncontrollably. When he was sufficiently recovered, he started running again.

Adding insult to injury, the police would not let him stop and rest for the last 10 miles since he was running next to a freeway. By the end of the race both of his big toenails had completely fallen off, but Emmerton had completed his 390-mile ordeal.

At the age of 50, this astounding athlete planned a 2,200-mile run from Perth on the west coast of Australia east across the barren Nullarbor Plain and then southeast to Melbourne. Emmerton eventually abandoned this idea, not because he would be crossing the worst desert in the world, but because he finally decided he wanted to get some fun out of his remaining years.

Apparently, he could not kick the running habit, however, for in December, 1975, he once again made a treacherous 50-mile run across Death Valley in an absurd race with the hustler-tennis player, Bobby Riggs. The challenge required that Riggs, aged 57, cover 25 miles while Emmerton, aged 56, would race 50 miles.

Emmerton proposed the idea 6 months prior to the event. His opponent was game although he admitted that the only running he ever did was "from the tennis court to the phone, from one hustle to the next, as is my nature." This would not be his first race, however, for two years prior he had been challenged to half the distance in the mile by Jim Ryun. Ryun ran a 4:03 . . . and lost!

Riggs prepared himself for Death Valley by training on the University of Nevada-Las Vegas track. Surrounded by groupies and tennis pros, he jogged a few miles each day while Emmerton put in 12 to 15 miles daily on the Dunes golf course.

On race day the air temperature was 69°F. (20.5°C.) and the ground temperature 95°F. (35°C.) at the starting point in Furnace Creek. The 25-mile course was out and back, requiring Emmerton to cover it twice. Emmerton set a fast pace from the start by averaging 7.5 minutes per mile for the first 16 miles. Riggs, assuming that he could walk the course in 8 hours and still win, turned on a smile and started to jog when he spotted his opponent approaching from the opposite direction. When Emmerton passed Riggs, the hustler was on his eighth mile and they were dead even. Riggs, the reporters, photographers, and publicity men, dressed in bright yellow outfits labeled "Sugar Daddy," passed around soft drinks and candy. They were followed by a deluxe house trailer over which Coca-Cola advertisements had been draped.

Emmerton ran alone followed only by his wife, Norma, in their blue Lincoln. Bill ran fast realizing that he had to push the pace to beat the 8-hour goal his opponent had set. The marathoner completed the first 25 miles in only 3½ hours. Just 10 miles later, however, the fast pace and low altitude (100 feet below sea level) started to take their toll.

When it was all over, Riggs gleefully tossed out candy and sprayed champagne at the finish line. He had won in a time of 8 hours 10 minutes but admitted that "playing Billie Jean was a cakewalk compared to this." His reward was a check from Sugar Daddy (Nabisco) for $1,000 a mile.

Emerton crossed the line exhausted in 8:51. He did not lose altogether, however, for he gained four new places in the *Guinness Book of World Records*: fastest 25 miles (3:30), 40 miles (6:37), 50 miles (8:51) in Death Valley and an age record. Retirement was again postponed as the two men talked of rematches for the next year in Iran, China, and Australia.

Elbow to elbow 1,705 runners take off from Hopkinton, Massachusetts in 1974 in the 77th annual Boston Marathon. This epic stampede attracts runners from all over the world, although the reward for the victor is nothing more than a laurel wreath and a gold medal.

8. Boston Marathon

A runner will find little loneliness in the Boston Marathon. This suburban stampede now consists of more than 1,500 entries each year and attracts about 250,000 spectators, one of the largest crowds for any athletic event in the world. As an epic race, it takes its place alongside such events as the Indianapolis 500, the Kentucky Derby, and Wimbledon.

This American tradition originated in 1897 with officials insisting that the race be free of professionalism, politics, and commercialism.

Sponsored by the Boston Athletic Association, it is held each April 19th on Patriot's Day, a state holiday celebrated with costumed minutemen and parades. The race begins in Hopkinton, halfway between Boston and Worcester, and ends in Boston. This marathon is the epitome of the amateur spirit, since the grand prize for the hours of grueling effort, physical exhaustion, and leg cramps is merely a laurel wreath and a gold medal. The next 34 finishers capture a small trophy or bronze medal, and everyone finishing under 4 hours is awarded a certificate stating his race time and placement.

The heart of the marathon, however, consists of the hundreds of amateurs attempting to conquer their own personal Mount Everests. These determined aspirants merely desire to complete the race, and their only material reward is a free bowl of beef stew and a podiatrist to treat their blisters.

Much has changed since John J. McDermott of New York won the first Boston Marathon in a little under 3 hours. Not only has the distance been lengthened to the standard 26 miles 385 yards and the record time slashed to less than 2 hours 10 minutes, but the number and variety of competitors continues to grow tremendously each year. In 1964, the record number of entrants was 250 and females were banned from entering. By 1970, there were five times as many athletes due to the great interest in jogging. In April, 1974, there were over 1,400 runners, and women had finally been accepted as official competitors.

Over 500 volunteers are now needed to conduct the race. Bostonians donate beef stew, locker space, and money, and all traffic is barred from the meandering 26-mile course. The importance of limiting all types of traffic was learned around the turn of the century when eight runners brazenly sprinted across the tracks in front of a 97-car freight train. While their opponents fumed and waited for the train to pass, those in front drew to an unbeatable lead. The officials, taking note of this unforeseen mishap, forced the railroads to arrange their schedules around the marathon thereafter.

Over the years the pack has become a potpourri of college students, doctors, priests, schoolteachers, and even the disabled. Each year many unofficial aspirants enter and even complete the race, thus attesting to the amateur spirit of this eccentric marathon. In 1970, Gene Roberts, a 24-year-old ex-Marine who had lost both legs in Vietnam, worked his wheelchair over the extremely hilly course and crossed the finish line 7 hours later.

In 1969, Alfred Ventrillo, a 62-year-old retired millworker, took about $4\frac{1}{2}$ hours to complete the race. He was blind and ran unofficially in order to show blind people what they are capable of doing. From 1966 on, husband-and-wife teams ran, defying the ban on females.

In recent years, the Boston Athletic Association has been forced to apply some new regulations in order to limit the size of the ever-growing pack of runners. In an attempt to eliminate the quacks and publicity seekers, a $2 entry fee has been imposed, and each entrant must now qualify for the race by completing another sanctioned marathon in the previous year in less than 3 hours. Men 40 years old and over and all women must complete one in less than $3\frac{1}{2}$ hours. (This rule was introduced prior to the 1976 marathon.)

On the morning of the race, all contestants proceed to the Hopkinton High School gymnasium where they present a physician's certificate or have a brief medical check-up. Most have loaded up on spaghetti the previous night since carbohydrates are essential for endurance events. Others swear by vitamins, wheat germ, and honey. As they proceed to the starting point, they spot helicopters buzzing overhead, kids perched in trees, photographers loaded down with equipment, and thousands of spectators lining the road. Many of the runners waste precious energy jockeying for a better position minutes before the race.

Finally, silence overtakes the crowd as the starter climbs a ladder and raises his gun. As it goes off, the pack surges forward, and a roar goes up from the mob of spectators. The runners' arms are thrust forward in self-defence, since anyone falling in the first mile is in serious trouble. It takes as much as a full minute for those in the rear of the pack to reach the starting line.

Eventually the runners string out, forming small groups, then finally breaking up many miles later. The crowds lining the roads cheer all who pass by. Children offer orange slices, and the runners down cups of electrolyte mixes while moving.

Although many competitors drop out throughout the race, the 20-mile point is the undoing of most. It is there that four hills culminate in the fearsome Heartbreak Hill. Not only is this hill long and steep, but it is encountered at the time when fatigue becomes a critical factor. Most good runners can complete 20 miles without serious problems, but the final 6 miles in a marathon eliminate many.

A throng of spectators congregate at the hill and, after consulting the program, cheer on many runners by name as they struggle up the long incline. There is a tremendous sense of empathy between the audience and the athletes at this point.

Many runners each year are unable to complete the race. Some collapse from exhaustion while others suffer severe muscle cramps. Those who do finish are often 10 pounds lighter than when they started and are badly dehydrated. In spite of the blisters, cramps, and dehydration, most will admit that they are running for the sheer joy and internal beauty that it brings. This is incomprehensible to the non-runner, but the ever-increasing number of amateur entrants each year in this and other marathons across the country is testimony to this statement.

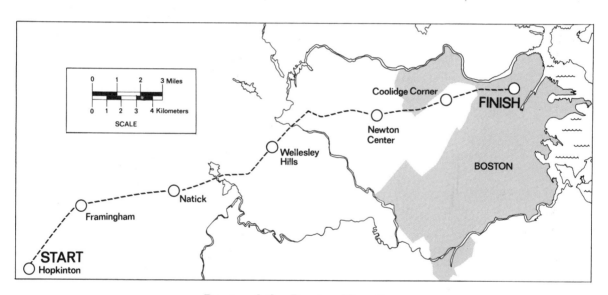

Route of the Boston Marathon.

9. Mr. Marathoner: Clarence DeMar

Undoubtedly, the greatest runner in the history of the Boston Marathon was Clarence DeMar, a native Bostonian. As a young boy, DeMar suffered from curvature of the spine and walked with an unnatural gait. He was forced to learn to use his legs at the age of 8 when his father died. Since his mother was burdened with six children and no income, the boy began walking the long, hilly roads to sell sewing notions door to door. To cover more territory, he soon developed a flat-footed, shuffling trot.

Clarence worked hard jogging through the snow that winter until he developed a severe infection on his ankle. The infection spread through his foot and was serious enough for amputation to be considered. Fortunately, it cleared up, and the boy was able to resume working and running the following summer.

When DeMar was 11, his family became destitute and was forced to separate. Clarence was sent to the Farm and Trades School, a state institution in Boston, where he studied hard but became quiet and withdrawn.

In 1907, Clarence entered the University of Vermont and took on two part-time jobs, one on the school's experimental farm and the other as an assistant in a print shop. True to form, he ran from one job to the other, totaling over 8 miles each day. He soon realized that he had the endurance to become a distance runner and, since he also admired the school athletes, he decided to try out for the track team.

The coach was appalled by Clarence's unconventional running style. His flat-footed shuffle and flailing arms were the epitome of bad form and yet he never tired. The coach was so impressed with his spirit and determination that he accepted him on the team.

Clarence learned much about racing strategy, but gave up trying to correct his form, since it decreased his speed. His first race was 4 miles, and he placed a respectable fourth. The coach would have made him a regular on the team, but Clarence was soon forced to leave school to support his family.

DeMar found a job, rented a house, and then sent for his mother, sisters, and brothers. Every day he ran from his house to his job in Boston and back again, a total of 14 miles. A friend joked that he should enter the Boston Marathon since he did so much running anyway. Clarence became interested and decided to see if he could cover the distance of 26 miles on a practice run.

Starting from home, he ran in the opposite direction from Boston. At the 10-mile point he was soaked in sweat and had been chased by dogs, but he felt good. When he had conquered 13 miles, he turned back toward his house. He was soon exhausted, his chest was heaving, and his legs felt dead. He was tempted to stop, but managed to reach home after covering 26 miles in just over 3 hours. Realizing that this was fast for a first attempt, Clarence planned a serious training program.

In February, 1910, he began running one 20-mile run each week in addition to the 14 miles each day to and from work. Clarence thoroughly examined the course on which the Boston Marathon was run, including the notorious Heartbreak Hill, the long, steep section 6 miles from the finish which is the ruin of many runners.

On April 19th, over 200 starters checked in at Ashland for the pre-race physical while thousands of spectators lined the sidelines awaiting the starting gun. DeMar found himself locked into the middle of the pack, where every runner was attempting to jockey for a better position. As the gun fired at noon, a roar exploded from the crowd.

The first mile was tightly bunched as usual, but before long the pack loosened as each runner found his own pace. Clarence conserved his energy by merely staying with the front third rather than fighting for an early lead. By using his knowledge of the course and his pre-race strategy, he shaved minutes off his time.

At the halfway point DeMar was about 7 minutes behind the lead runners. As he reached and started up Heartbreak Hill, he slowed somewhat while trying to ignore the crowd cheering along the roadside. He made it over the hill easily and finally had Boston in sight. DeMar was now in fourth place advancing on third. Streaking down Commonwealth Avenue he stole second place from a Canadian. Now only Freddy Cameron was between him and the finish line.

As they turned into Exeter Street, DeMar summoned his last energy reserves for a final push; however, he was unable to close the gap between him and the leader. Freddy Cameron crossed the finish in a time of 2 hours 28 minutes. Clarence DeMar shuffled over the line only one minute later. The public loved Clarence and was amazed to see a novice place second when over half the entrants could not even finish.

DeMar ran the usual 14 miles to and from work the very next day although sore and tired. He soon received invitations to various track meets but only attended those that cost him no more than a half-day's pay. He enjoyed marathons much more than these shorter races and was already planning for the next April 19th.

In the autumn, he stopped competing and trained seriously for the marathon. DeMar thrived on strenuous training and ran more than 100 miles each week.

At the next Boston Marathon, Clarence was no longer a novice and many people recognized him. During the pre-race physical, however, the doctor found a slight heart murmur and strongly advised him not to race. DeMar pleaded with the physician that he had run every day since he was 8 years old and that training was more physically punishing than the race itself.

The doctor agreed to let him race if Clarence would drop out if he got into trouble. Terribly upset, DeMar started the race raggedly. He continued to run poorly for 3 miles but concentrated hard and eventually smoothed out his rhythm. By blocking out thoughts of the doctor and the noisy spectators, he remembered and followed his pre-race plan.

He started up Heartbreak Hill in fourth place and reached the top in second. DeMar virtually flew down the other side, and at that point went into first place. He maintained the lead all the way into Boston, down Commonwealth Avenue, into Exeter Street, and across the finish line. The second place runner was a full half-mile behind. Clarence set a new marathon world record time of 2 hours 21 minutes 39 seconds. The fans idolized this great athlete in particular because he had overcome his twisted spine and abnormal heart by unfailing determination and drive.

DeMar was chosen to be on the U.S. track team in the 1912 Olympics in Stockholm, Sweden. The coaches tried to change Clarence's running style by insisting he run on his toes and stop swinging his arms sideways.

On the day of the marathon, 68 Olympians lined up at the starting line under a scorching

July sun. The thick dust and sweltering heat took a drastic toll. A Portuguese runner collapsed at the halfway point and was rushed to a hospital where he later died. DeMar could bear the heat, dust, and fatigue, but not the new running style forced on him by his coaches. A South African, Kenneth McArthur, won the race, and 10 others finished ahead of Clarence. He vowed never again to alter his running form.

Running brought DeMar fame and, along with it, invitations to address civic groups, to officiate at track meets, and to participate in races all over the world. Throughout all this, Clarence attended classes at Harvard, taught Sunday School, became a scoutmaster, and held a regular job. Although he learned to enjoy life, his running suffered. He continued running the 14 miles to and from work but did little competitive training.

As a soldier during World War I, DeMar was sent to France. He tried to train while running in his army boots and often had to convince the M.P.'s he was not running away. After the war he returned to competitive running and won the 1922 Boston Marathon. The fans loved him more than ever since he was now 34 and yet had set another marathon world record in a time of 2 hours 18 minutes 10 seconds.

In 1923, DeMar was bed-ridden for an entire month due to a severe illness. He was told not to race that year, but he ignored the doctor's warning. After training intensively, he went on to win the 1923 Boston Marathon.

In 1924, DeMar became the first runner ever to win the Boston classic four times. He was also selected for the U.S. Olympic team that year and this time refused to let the coaches change his running form. In that marathon there were 58 starters from 19 nations. DeMar earned the nickname, "Old Man of Marathoning," since at 36 he was 10 to 15 years older than most of the other athletes in the Olympics. He placed third and was only one minute behind the second-place runner with a time of 2 hours 48 minutes 14 seconds.

DeMar's friends advised him to retire due to his age and his questionable heart. He ignored them and proceeded to take second place in the 1925 Boston Marathon. In 1926, he won the 20-mile Sesquicentennial Marathon from Valley Forge to Philadelphia. He also placed third in that year's Boston classic. In 1927, he won the Providence Marathon in Rhode Island, and for the fifth time won the Boston Marathon.

In March, 1928, DeMar entered the St. Patrick's Day Providence-to-Boston run, a distance of 44 miles. He maintained a $7\frac{1}{2}$-mile-per-hour pace and won in less than 6 hours. That year he earned his sixth Boston Marathon victory and a place for the third time on the U.S. Olympic team. His team members were in awe of him, but in Amsterdam, Holland, he had one of his greatest disappointments. He wanted to bring America her first Olympic marathon victory in 20 years. He also knew this was to be his last Olympic race. Out of a field of 72 starters, DeMar placed 27th. He was now regarded as the grand "old man" of long-distance running.

He would not retire, however, and in the fall of 1928 won a 25-mile run in Halifax, Nova Scotia, against 40 Canadians. In 1930, at the age of 42, DeMar won the Boston Marathon for the seventh time, won the Port Chester (New York) Marathon—and got married. At that time he moved to Keene, New Hampshire, and became the assistant director of physical education and an instructor in printing at the Keene Normal School.

At the age of 44, DeMar also became a part-time graduate student at Boston University. True to form, he commuted the 90 miles from Keene to Boston once a week by a combination of running and hitching rides. He would jog from Keene's city limits and after 2 hours of running, would start thumbing rides. Never once was he late for class. On the return trip, he invariably was stopped by constables as he was running through the streets late at night. Finally reaching home at 3 or 4 a.m., he would sleep a few hours, and then go to work. In

Clarence DeMar crosses the finish line of the Boston Marathon in 1930 for his seventh win. "Mr. Marathoner" earned his nickname after completing his 34th Boston run in 1954 at the age of 66. He never stopped running until the year before his death at 70. Hard to believe that this titan of marathoning was born with curvature of the spine.

addition to all of this, Clarence continued to run competitively.

In 1954, at the astounding age of 66, DeMar ran his 34th Boston Marathon before a cheering crowd of 500,000 spectators. They urged him on with chants of "Mr. Marathoner" until he finally crossed the finish, placing a respectable 78th out of 133 starters. DeMar's final race was in 1957 at 69 years of age when he competed in a 15-km. (9.4-mile) race at Bath, Maine. Unbelievably, he placed 14th out of 50

runners. The following year, at the age of 70, Clarence DeMar died.

During his career, DeMar competed in more than 1,000 long-distance races, held the U.S. national marathon championship longer than anyone, and won the Boston Marathon seven times. After his death, a team of doctors made an exhaustive study of DeMar's heart. They found that he had atherosclerosis, cardiac enlargement, and arteries in his heart which were three times the normal diameter.

"K. Switzer" entered the Boston Marathon and was almost shouldered out of the race by crusty official Jock Semple. Fellow runner and unofficial bodyguard, Thomas Miller, threw a block that tossed Semple out of the running, however, and Kathy Switzer sped on to the finish. This was 1967 when females were banned.

10. The Plight of the Female Runner

In 1966, the king of the Boston Marathon was Japan's Kenji Kimihara who completed the race in 2 hours 17 minutes 11 seconds. For the first time in the history of the race, however, there was also an unofficial queen of the marathon, a leggy blond from Winchester, Massachusetts, named Roberta Gibb Bingay.

Roberta had started running a few years previously in order to keep her husband company. She grew to love running and began training regularly. When her husband decided to enter the 1966 Boston Marathon, Roberta learned that women were barred from the race. She rebelled and conjured up a plan to join the race unofficially.

On the day of the race she hid in the bushes near the starting line in Hopkinton. After the main pack of runners had passed by and disappeared, she leaped onto the course. Clad in a hooded blue sweatshirt, she went undetected at first, but eventually, as the day grew warmer she was forced to strip down to a swim suit and a pair of shorts.

Roberta completed the race in a very respectable 3 hours 21 minutes 2 seconds. Although she placed a remarkable 124th out of an all-male field of 416, Will Cloney, the director of the marathon, refused to recognize that she even ran. To do so would have demolished the theory that women were not capable of running a marathon.

In 1967, a 19-year-old college student from Syracuse University became the first woman to obtain an official number and complete the race as well. Kathy Switzer's application was unwittingly accepted by the B.A.A. since she had signed it merely K. Switzer.

The day of the race was cold and rainy so Kathy did not appear unusual dressed in a hooded sweatshirt. After the race was under way and she removed the hood, the press realized that a woman was officially entered in the race. Jock Semple, the marathon's co-director, was furious. The balding Scotsman firmly believed that she had desecrated the race. The wirephotos coming from Boston on that April 19th carried a classic picture of a fiery-eyed old man (Semple) grinding his teeth and clutching at the number 261 on the back of a track sweat suit (Switzer's). To Semple's left was burly Tom Miller, a hammer thrower as well as Kathy's boyfriend. In the next photograph we see Miller giving Semple a hefty shoulder-block and knocking him off the course. With the help of her powerful body-guard, Kathy finished the race in about $4\frac{1}{2}$ hours. Roberta Bingay again entered the race unofficially and completed it in the excellent time of 3 hours 27 minutes 17 seconds.

After that race the Amateur Athletic Union banned Kathy Switzer and all other females from competing with men. Ever since 1967 Kathy has been striving to earn respect for women in sports. She is trying to eradicate the tendency for women to be thought of as women first and athletes second. Kathy's greatest accomplishment has been in successfully fighting the A.A.U.'s ruling against women. In 1972, she finally ran in the Boston Marathon officially and legally.

Kathy as well as other female athletes realize that they have a long way to go before the public accepts women in athletics. She recalls her first Boston Marathon: As she reached the exhausting and critical 20-mile point, she looked up to see an elderly couple watching her. She observed the woman clapping and smiling, and assumed it was in admiration of her stamina and determination. As Kathy passed by, however, she heard the woman exclaim to her husband, "Look, Dearie, isn't that cute. It's a girl and she's wearing earrings!"

Times have changed since Elaine Peterson ran in the 1968 Boston Marathon after having a male friend take the required medical exam for her. Since 1972, Elaine and any other qualified woman have been free to enter the race.

11. Mr. Boston Marathon

Jock Semple is the indispensable, unpaid coach and trainer of the Boston Athletic Association. He processes thousands of applications, answers a flood of correspondence, and even herds the runners onto the field on the day of the Boston Marathon. Believing that this race is second in importance only to the Olympic Games, he makes certain that rules and regulations are followed to the letter.

Ever since the late 1960's, however, he has mainly been fighting for the dignity of the race. Although the best runners from all over the world still come to Boston each April, more and more eccentrics also show up each year. Publicity hounds, fraternity brothers, fat people, and women send Jock Semple into a flying rage.

In spite of Boston's absolute dependency on Semple for the race, he has become the marathon's heavy, due to the Kathy Switzer incident. He was outraged that she had obtained an official number by having a doctor send in a health certificate under the name K. Switzer, thus waiving the pre-race physical. In speaking of Roberta Gibb Bingay, he refers to the blue-eyed blond as the "Gibb dame." She never even bothered to get a number but always ran well.

Jock explains that he is not really opposed to women's athletics, but believes that everyone must respect the amateur rules. In the late 1960's these rules stated that women could not race more than $1\frac{1}{2}$ miles. Semple was firmly convinced that even if their races were length-ened, they had no place competing with men. He snarled that it was unthinkable for a woman to run with the famous Jim Ryun!

Jock used to run in the Boston Marathon each year until, at the age of 46, he decided his work as an official did not allow for enough training time. Each morning at 8:30 a.m. he runs a mile and a half in the Boston Garden. He works next door in an office cluttered with trophies, mugs, and loving cups.

As a registered physical therapist, he gives expert massages while answering phone inquiries about the race. He continually berates the college students from M.I.T., Tufts, and Harvard, but has nothing but praise for the genuine runners.

On the day of the marathon, Semple rises at 6 a.m. and drives to the Prudential Building in Back Bay, Boston where he distributes the checkpoint signs to his aids. He herds all the runners onto the buses and has them taken to Hopkinton for the start of the race.

Once Semple arrives at the starting line, he stations the best 25 runners in front of the pack. At noon when the gun is fired, Jock jumps into the press bus and proceeds to chase after the jokers, oddballs, and eccentrics dressed in costumes. To him the marathon is sacred and he will not stand for anyone desecrating it. In one race a man ran in an Uncle Sam costume, bearing an advertisement for storm windows on his back. Semple ran next to him while continually throwing cups of water in his face. One year he tried to kick a dog off the course, and in another race Semple charged at a runner who was wearing swim fins and an absurd mask. Jock missed him and landed in a gutter. In that embarrassing incident, the police attempted to arrest the disgruntled official for attempted assault.

Acting as a self-appointed trainer for all the serious entrants in the marathon, Semple greets them at the finish line by slapping a blanket around them and sending them into the building for a check-up and his free bowl of beef stew. He impatiently waits until the last man finishes while continually swearing that he can walk the course in 4 hours 45 minutes—and yet some lunatics take 7 hours.

Jock insisted that the B.A.A. limit the field of entries in order to eliminate the oddballs and cater to the serious runners who train so relentlessly for this annual event. He achieved this: runners now have to qualify in the year prior to the race in order to be official competitors. The Boston Marathon was one of the last races typifying pure amateurism and allowing anyone to race with the world's best. Whether these recent restrictions will alter the nature of the race is yet to be seen.

In any case, Jock Semple, forever grinding his teeth and hotly arguing with cops in his thick brogue, is unquestionably the backbone of the Boston Marathon.

12. The Race That Went to the Dogs

Awaiting the start of the 1961 Boston Marathon, spectators bundled up in sweaters and coats to ward off the 38°F. (3.3°C.) chill. Among the 166 starters, the Finns were favored to win since they had captured first place in the Boston classic five times in the previous 8 years. In 1959, Eino Oksanen, a chunky, pink-skinned Helsinki detective, had won the epic marathon, and was entered this year again. Only one American since 1945 had won this race. John J. Kelley, a 30-year-old Groton, Connecticut, schoolteacher, had won in 1957, but usually placed a strong second. He has been runner-up four times since 1956. He, too, was starting in 1961.

As a light snow began falling on the wintery April day in 1961, Kelley and Oksanen lined up at the starting point. Also in the pack that day was the unknown 39-year-old British coal miner, Fred Norris. Norris was then a freshman at McNeese State College in Louisiana and was entering his first Boston Marathon.

Kelley and Oksanen quickly shook off early challengers as the race got under way. Their greatest obstacle, however, was a flop-eared black mongrel that ran with them for 14 miles. The dog incessantly nipped at their heels while darting back and forth across the road and eluding frustrated State Troopers.

With only 10 miles to go, Kelley, Oksanen, and Norris ran close together preparing for the strenuous 5-mile climb up the Newton Hills. Suddenly, the dog charged out from the left-hand side of the road and swerved into the runners. Oksanen quickly jumped to avoid him, but the mongrel hit Kelley hard across the legs.

The great runner sprawled violently onto the road and badly skinned his legs, arms, hands, and face. It happened so suddenly that the press bus almost ran over him. Norris stopped immediately, turned back, and shouted at Kelley to get up. When Kelley appeared dazed and unable to move, Norris lifted him to his feet, forcing him to snap out of his trance. The wounded runner immediately re-entered the race, but both had lost valuable time.

They had also lost the essential steady, trance-like pace that distance runners fall into, carrying them beyond the painful muscle cramps and blisters. Prior to the accident, Norris had been running with a normally incapacitating stitch in his left side. Stopping to help Kelley hurt his running critically.

As the three climbed the hills leading into Boston, Norris slowed down. The race was then between Oksanen and Kelley. Kelley took the lead with the Finn staying a half stride behind the leader's shoulder, using him as a windbreak.

Merely 1,000 yards from the finish, Oksanen suddenly pulled in front like a tank. Kelley desperately fought to stay with him, but the Finn won by 125 yards, crossing the finish only 25 seconds ahead of Kelley. The winning time was 2 hours 23 minutes 29 seconds. The 25 seconds was one of the narrowest margins in 65 years of the Boston race.

The hero that day, however, was Fred Norris who came in third and was cheered and praised by all. Kelley admitted that he was not sure that he could have put on such a great show of sportsmanship himself. Norris wryly commented that someone should have shot that blasted dog.

Oksanen later explained his victories by saying, "In Finland, we don't ride around in automobiles like you do over here. There, everybody runs."

13. The Hunky Bunch

If not the fastest, the most unusual marathon runners in modern history are probably the Chun family. The children range in age from 9 to 15 while the parents are 41 and 45. The family competes in races anywhere from Hawaii to Boston and wears sweatshirts emblazoned with the phrase, "THE HUNKY BUNCH." Their team is made up of Dr. and Mrs. Hing Hua Chun and six children: Jerry, May Lynne, Hinky, June, Joy, and Daven, all members of the Pacific Road Runners Club.

Dr. Chun, a distinguished internist and cardiologist, is the chief of medicine at St. Francis Hospital, Honolulu, and an associate professor at the University of Hawaii. The name, "Hunky Bunch," grew out of a nickname Dr. Chun's Honolulu classmates gave him. They could not remember Hing Hua, so they merely called him Hunky. The name stuck as is evidenced by the listing in the phone book, "Chun, Dr. H. H. Hunky," and by his license plate which reads "Hunky."

Dr. Chun met his second wife, Connie, in 1970 while she was vacationing in Honolulu. Connie, born on the island of Panay in the Philippines, had been a nurse. At the age of 28 she was awarded a Fulbright Scholarship in nursing and attended Loma Linda University in California. She later obtained her masters degree at the University of Hawaii. Before her marriage to Hunky, Connie lived in San Francisco with her three daughters. Now, at the age of 45, the 5-foot-2-inch, 104-pound Connie is planning to study law.

Dr. Chun, a third-generation native Hawaiian, lived in Honolulu with his three sons from a previous marriage. Rounding out the cosmopolitan flavor of the household, the boys are an even mixture of Chinese and Japanese. Hunky was intensely interested in preventive heart-attack therapy and gave up his avid tennis playing for jogging. The 6-foot-1-inch doctor had never taken up sports in high school, at the University of Hawaii, nor at Northwestern University where he obtained his medical credentials.

The first member of his family to join him in jogging was 11-year-old Jerry. The year that Connie and Hunky met was also the year that Jerry first began running competitively, setting a precedent that the entire family was soon to follow. Connie jokes that she was angry when her new husband started running, but when all the kids joined in, she did too.

The innocent jogging quickly turned competitive, so much so that the walls of their house are now covered with ribbons and trophies. Even little Daven, the youngest member of the family, held ten world marks for ages 8 and 9 in distances from 2 miles to the marathon. Although all the records cannot be listed here, the family collection of Hawaiian, U.S., and world records now numbers more than 60.

In December, 1973, the entire family except for Connie entered the A.A.U. Rim of the Pacific Marathon in Honolulu. It was the first marathon they had ever entered and probably

Dr. Hing Hua "Hunky" Chun of Hawaii and two of his daughters, May and Joy, happily participating in the 1974 Boston Marathon. Four other members of the "Bunch" also joined in, all through the courtesy of the American Medical Joggers Association, which cut the qualifying red tape to permit the family to run.

the best family showing in history. Jerry at 14 years old turned in a remarkable 3 hours 9 minutes 20 seconds. Hinky at 13 completed the course in 3:13:39. Daven, 9, was only a few minutes behind with a 3:19:01. This incredible time beat the world age group record by 9 minutes. June, 14, was a mere 40 seconds over the U.S. women's age group record with a time of 3:25:31. These four family members broke the 3:30:0 time barrier and therefore, would have qualified for the upcoming Boston Marathon if they had been old enough. May Lynne, 15, clocked an excellent time of 3:43:09 while Joy, 13, came in at 3:46:51. Dr. Chun, 41, was right behind with a 3:48:23.

After their first highly successful family marathon, the Hunky Bunch was invited by the American Medical Joggers Association to run in the 1974 Boston Marathon. None of them would have qualified technically, since to enter they had to be 19 years old or over *and* have run a marathon in the previous year in less than 3:30:0.

The Chun household operates under the admirable philosophy of the cultivation of both mind and body. All of the children are on their school honor roll except Daven whose school does not have one.

The family is run democratically with everyone having a say. Connie and Hunky share the cooking while the entire group shares the housework. The only problem which seems to arise from all this is that Connie and her daughters are Seventh Day Adventists and, therefore, have trouble with Saturday track meets.

Dr. and Mrs. Chun do not believe in pushing their children, but merely in setting examples for them. They are only to compete as long as they want to and as long as it does not affect their schoolwork. Connie and Hunky firmly believe that although running provides endurance, scholarship provides careers. Furthermore, the doctor realizes that running will expand their cardiovascular systems and that such beneficial effects will remain to help them later in life.

Every evening the family takes off on a 2-hour run across Keehi Lagoon Park and over the hills of Tantalus Drive. Another beneficial result of all this exercise is that the children burn off so much energy that they rarely fight among each other. In addition to being a record-breaking team on foot, the Hunky Bunch's family devotion and gung-ho morale make for a standout team in the home as well.

14. Mountain Marathons

One of the greatest distance mountain-runners of this century is a 40-year-old farmer from Bowerdale, England. Joss Naylor conditions his mind and lean 135-pound body in a very unconventional manner. In addition to making extraordinary mountain runs, known as fell-running in Britain, Naylor single-handedly farms 150 acres of mountainous sheep-grazing land.

Fell-running first became popular in England's Lake District more than a century ago, and is one of the most strenuous tests of endurance in the vast realm of athletics. The runner must plod through peaty bog patches and high grass and then conquer unbearable changes in gradient over such terrain as loose stone and rock outcroppings.

In June, 1974, Naylor completed a brutal crossing of the Pennine Chain, a mountainous stretch from Scotland to the peak district of Derbyshire, in the Midlands of England. He ran a total distance of 271.5 miles and did it entirely alone!

He set out from Kirk Yethold in Scotland at about 3 a.m. and ran well the first day. He tore a muscle in his groin, however, and by the next morning was unable to lift his leg. In spite of this painful handicap, Naylor continued on by applying deep heat and then dragging his leg. The second morning out he discovered that he had strained his Achilles tendon. These injuries were added to a back problem he had suffered previously while baling hay. To top off this "comedy of errors," Naylor had knocked his hip out of its socket a few weeks before the start of the run, and it was still sore.

By the third day Naylor was in terrible pain but was determined to finish. By the time he did complete the run, his ankles and hands had swelled up, his shoulders ached, and his legs felt dead. He completed the 271.5-mile run and 32,000-foot ascent and descent, however, in 3 days 4 hours and 36 seconds, beating the previous record by 24 hours. This time included rest stops totaling 18 hours 43 minutes.

Naylor was deeply disappointed in spite of his new record, since he had wanted to finish in less than 3 days. The run took its toll on him physically since he was unable to sleep well for many nights after, and it took 6 months for his legs to recover completely.

Naylor's medical history certainly did not indicate he had the stuff of which great runners are made. In addition to being very small as a child, he was kicked in the back at the age of 9 and suffered a permanently damaged spine. After bearing the pain for 11 years, he finally had two spinal discs removed.

When he was 23, Naylor leaped over a wire fence and fell, smashing his back against a rock. Two years passed before that injury healed.

Living among the misty, cold mountains in the Lake District, he found many steep hillsides on which to train. On the peaks, which shot straight up from the green, idyllic valleys, about ten tourists were killed by falls each year.

Naylor, at 32, finally began serious fell-running. There had been no organized running offered at school, and he had never attempted a flat race or a marathon. After setting his first record in June, 1970, he went on to break 12 more in the next 5 years.

One of Naylor's feats involved running the classic "Lakeland 24 hours." This race was conceived in 1864 when the Reverend J. M. Elliott conquered four mountains in 8½ hours. Others continued to break this record until in 1903, Dr. A. W. Wakefield determined that the goal would be to run up the greatest number of peaks above 2,000 feet and return to the starting point within 24 hours.

The first record (which lasted 28 years) was established in 1932 by Bob Graham. He conquered 42 peaks by ascending a total of 27,000 feet in 23 hours 39 minutes. By 1965, a record of 60 peaks was set. In 1971, Joss Naylor squeezed in 61 mountain ascents and, in 1972, increased the number to 63.

Naylor, however, rarely being satisfied, was determined to create an unsurpassable record in this event. On June 22, 1975, he set out at 7 a.m. from the base of Skiddaw Mountain. The first section of the course was filled with tall grass, heather, and dangerous potholes. In spite of the rough terrain and intense heat, he ran well. Too well, in fact, since he reached the first checkpoint before his pacers even had his drink ready.

Due to his eventual dehydration and electrolyte imbalance, Naylor suffered from severe muscle cramps. He continued on, however, climbing up jagged rocks and running over loose scree, or rocky debris. When darkness fell, the dangers increased greatly. The full moon and the flashlights carried by the pacers created a confusing double shadow. With the coming of dawn, Naylor regained his rhythm and made good time. When it was all over, he had climbed 40,000 feet and covered 108 miles in 24 hours. He had set a new record of 72 summits in 23 hours 11 minutes. After this grueling, exhausting feat, Joss rested only two days and returned to his demanding ranch work.

Naylor is unique in that he does not believe in earning money from sports. He refuses to run in professional races, but did accept money from friends in order to travel to Colorado for the two-way Pikes Peak Marathon. He arrived several weeks early in order to adjust to the altitude and prepare for the most strenuous marathon in the world.

Two days prior to the race, Naylor inspected the course by riding to the 14,110-foot summit on a cogwheel train. From the top he could see part of the narrow trail curving through boulders and barren slopes of shale. About 1,000 feet below the summit, there is a 1,500-foot drop, known as the Cirque, which was carved out by an ancient glacier. Beneath this, the lower sections of the mountain are blanketed with blue spruce. Colorado Springs lies at the bottom and the plains of Kansas extend beyond.

Naylor, in spite of preparing for this unpredictable race by running above 4,000 feet in Scotland and 9,000 feet in Switzerland, was now extremely dizzy at the summit of this great Colorado mountain. The week prior to the event, Naylor jogged up the torturous 13-mile trail three times. On Tuesday he jogged for 3 hours but was forced to walk the remaining 2,000 feet. On Wednesday Naylor made it in 2 hours 40 minutes, and on Thursday, he ran for 2 hours 15 minutes, stopping at 13,000 feet.

At this point he realized he would not adjust to the altitude in time and, therefore, would not beat the local entrants. He did not mind, however, as long as he finished with a respectable time. Naylor's main interest was in helping fell-running to become an international sport.

Pikes Peak is said to have been discovered in 1806 by Lieutenant Zebulon M. Pike of the U.S. Army. He attempted an ascent but, when stopped by deep snow, he exclaimed that no mortal man would ever climb it. Undoubtedly, the Ute Indians had climbed the mountain many years previously, and 14 years after Pike's failure, three men officially conquered it.

Between 1921 and 1923 a determined entrepreneur, Fred Barr, plowed and shoveled his

It's 13 miles up and 13 miles down the dizzying 14,110-foot-high Pikes Peak Marathon course, considered by many to be the most strenuous in the world.

way to the 10,200-foot point where he planned to set up business. He built Barr Camp and led tourists on burros up to the cabins. The first foot race up the mountainside was in 1936 and the first marathon originated in August, 1956.

Indefatigable Rudy Fahl organizes the marathon as an annual event. Rudy has made the strenuous ascent 140 times, including 13 races, but at the age of 77 declines to compete anymore.

Mt. Manitou, dotted with scrub oak, is the first obstacle in the race. The runners quench their thirst at French Creek and then pick up the pace as they pass through aspen and blue spruce on level ground. Upon reaching the halfway point, Barr Camp, the competitors can see Pikes Peak for the first time. At this point the trail becomes painfully steep and is laden with 2 miles of tortuous switchbacks.

Eventually, the runners come upon Dismal Forest, a graveyard of scorched tree trunks burned mercilessly 50 years before.

Trees are left behind at the timberline of 12,000 feet and only rocks and snow come into view. A bronze plaque has been placed here in memory of Mrs. G. Inestine B. Roberts who in 1957 at the age of 88 made her 14th and final ascent. She died of exposure on the return trip to the bottom. The remainder of the trail consists of steep, murderous switchbacks called "16 Golden Stairs."

A total of 350 hopefuls entered the classic race in 1975. The motley group was made up of an assortment of runners, joggers, and hikers that included 35 women. The favorite was a 27-year-old geologist, Rick Trujillo, from Ouray, Colorado.

Trujillo had a tremendous advantage in that he worked above 9,000 feet at Camp Bird Mine. He already had proven his great running ability by winning the marathon twice previously and setting a round-trip record of 3:36:40. Other notables that year were Chuck Smead, a 24-year-old Californian, who wanted to break his old record to the summit of 2:07:38. Walt Stack, at 67, was also entered. This San Franciscan had won in his age group four times and had earned the nickname "Iron Man." The honor of being the oldest competitor, however, was awarded to 83-year-old Lady Brenda Ueland from Minneapolis.

The day of the race was sunny and the highway was crowded with spectators driving to the summit. The first runner to the top, as expected, was Trujillo who set a new ascent record of 2:01:47. After breaking Smead's previous record by almost 6 minutes, Trujillo turned and started back down. Naylor, suffering badly from the altitude, staggered to the summit in 18th place in 2 hours 41 minutes 5 seconds. Exhausted and defeated, he sat down and drank the English equivalent of Gatorade, called Acolade. Immediately revived, he leaped to his feet and sprinted down the trail.

Trujillo reached the bottom in the record time of 3:31:05. Naylor trotted across the finish 36 minutes 17 seconds later, in sixth place. In spite of the blood pounding in his head and the overwhelming feeling of exhaustion, he heartily shook hands with Trujillo and the two great runners shared their mutual respect.

15. America's Fastest Olympian: Frank Shorter

In 1972, Frank Shorter became the first American since 1908 to win the Olympic marathon. He did so by reaching and maintaining a pace which was faster than he had ever previously experienced in his life. Shorter blazed through the final 9 miles in Munich at an astounding speed of 4 minutes 45 seconds per mile.

Even more amazing is that Shorter completed the race in spite of severe liver cramps caused by sugar insufficiency, or hypoglycemia. Although the cramps occur regularly when Frank runs, he stoically denies the pain, preferring instead to view the sport as romantic and sensual. This young athlete explains that during the marathon such pain may not be noticeable since the mind becomes blurred. The runner focuses mainly on the battle against slowing down.

Ironically, the gold medal winner bears only contempt for athletes who take the sport too seriously or focus on a single goal. To him the marathon is an experience which runners share with each other as opposed to being merely a time trial. The marathon forces each athlete to go beyond the normal limits of his body and often to maintain the fastest pace he can physically bear, for an extended period of time. This unique, superhuman feat is known as "redlining" and sets marathon runners apart from most other athletes.

While the swimmers in Munich were swearing that they never wanted to see a pool again

Frank Shorter crosses the finish line at the Munich Olympic Stadium in 1972, after running the last half of the race completely alone!

once their race was over, the distance runners were out on the track the very next day. For example, the day following Shorter's historic performance, he ran 5 miles, and the day after that he did 20!

For this 5-foot-11-inch, 130-pound runner the sport is 98 per cent training and 2 per cent competition. In one 5-year period he missed only 6 days of running. In the winter, Frank dons thermal underwear, thermal socks, and sometimes even goggles. He submits to wearing long pants only in extreme cold. Running is so much a part of his life that during airport layovers, he quickly changes into his track suit and runs on the feeder roads. If he occasionally gets sick, he omits only one of his twice-daily workouts.

Shorter, like many other distance runners, is intelligent and articulate. Marathon runners may develop these attributes to a higher degree than other athletes since their sport gives them so much time to think. Shorter, for instance, averages 140 miles a week and, at times, has done more than 200 miles. In order to handle such long hours of running, the athlete must have the ability to deal mentally with "empty" time. In the race itself a trance may set in, making the event seem shorter than it really is. This mental state also helps the athlete become oblivious to pain.

Since the ability to deal with extreme mental and physical demands requires great maturity, most marathon runners are over 30 years old. Frank Shorter, however, earned his medal at the relatively young age of 25. Reaching that point was not easy, since Frank suffered growing pains in acquiring his abilities.

As an undergraduate at Yale, he had reached a plateau as an uninspired 2-miler. Suddenly, at the end of his senior year he began running twice a day instead of only once. This simple change cut his recovery time in half and bettered his time for longer distances. The first time he clocked himself in a distance run, he found that he had covered 6 miles in a fast 29 minutes. That June he entered a 6-mile N.C.A.A. race and won although only 2 months prior to that he would not even have attempted it.

In the fall, Shorter entered the University of New Mexico medical school and reduced his workouts to only 7 miles a day. Soon afterward a family crisis arose when Frank's father was forced to return to New York to resume his medical practice which had failed in Taos. Shorter soon found himself taking a leave of absence from school to return home to care for his nine brothers and sisters. As he later explained, he finally encountered a long overdue identity crisis once he was out of school. He decided that medicine was not for him and that he would move to Boulder, Colorado, as soon as his father returned home. He wanted to be near his girl friend and future wife, Louise, and also to find out once and for all how good he was as a runner.

After Frank moved to Boulder, he began twice-daily workouts, totaling 15 miles. By that spring he was running 20 miles each day in Gainesville, Florida, with Jack Batchelor, one of the top distance runners in the country. At the same time he entered the University of Florida law school.

When Shorter found his recovery time dropping remarkably, he realized that he now had the endurance to complete a marathon. His first race was quite a test. On a blazing 90°F. (32°C.) day in Cali, Colombia, he entered the Pan Am Marathon. In spite of the 4,000-foot elevation and a one-minute emergency stop in a cornfield, Shorter won the strenuous race by 4 minutes in a time of 2 hours 22 minutes. Kenny Moore, another great U.S. distance runner, collapsed from heat prostration.

Shorter went on to win the next four marathons that he entered. In addition, he showed great versatility by setting U.S. records for both the 2-mile indoor and the 10,000-meter outdoor races. The highlight of his astounding career, however, was his gold medal victory in the 1972 Olympic marathon. That coveted prize had not been captured by an American in 64 years!

II. THE DISTANCE SWIMMER

Gertrude Ederle

16. The Proving Ground: The English Channel

Historically, the unpredictable, 22-mile channel between Dover, England, and Calais, France, has been the foremost maker of swimmers' reputations, in spite of also being the busiest shipping lane in the world. In addition to huge freighters bearing down on him, the swimmer must contend with violent weather, powerful currents, jellyfish, and chilling water temperatures between 57° and 62°F. (14° and 16.6°C.).

However, the most common causes of failure in this stretch of water are weather and seasickness. Storm fronts move swiftly and violently over the Channel, taking the swimmer and crew by surprise. Sometimes an entire season, July to September, passes by without one acceptable day for the swim. Since food is vital for supplying the enormous amount of energy needed for the event, it is essential that the swimmer keep it down. The turbulent, churning seas, however, make seasickness a constant threat.

Cramps, too, are always a danger since the athlete is never allowed to touch his escort boat. There is always an official observer on board to disqualify him in such a case. Swimmers do not even hang onto their boat at feeding time but receive their food in a net attached to a 5-foot pole.

The powerful currents, however, were probably the greatest hazard to the earlier swimmers, and it was many decades before they learned to time their departures to avoid an opposing ebb or flood tide. For instance, a swimmer crossing from France to England must start from Cape Gris-Nez on the last 2 hours of the southwesterly ebb tide. If he swims northwest, he actually is carried west. Then the flood tide takes over, pushing the swimmer north for $5\frac{1}{2}$ hours. At this point he is southwest of the notorious Goodwin Sands, the graveyard of countless ships, including the Spanish Armada.

Then for the next 2 hours the swimmer tries to get as close to the coast as possible before the ebb tide starts again. If he is in the vicinity of the coastline, the southwesterly flowing ebb tide carries him into land. If the swimmer is too far offshore, however, he is carried helplessly downstream away from his goal and is unable to land. A good navigator piloting the escort boat is essential.

Over the years swimmers have learned to take advantage of the twice-monthly neap tides whenever possible. During these 5-day periods the currents are slower, making a crossing easier. Frequently, such advantages are denied by foul weather.

The First Crossings

Strangely enough, the first crossing of the treacherous strip of water was merely a prank. In 1862, an Englishman named Hoskins successfully floated on a bundle of straw from England to France. With the idea implanted, others

Fighting nausea resulting from a jellyfish sting, Matthew Webb accepts a bottle of brandy in his second and successful attempt to cross the bitter-cold nightwaters of the English Channel on August 24, 1875.

eventually tried to swim across the same waterway.

One of the first to try the crossing was an Englishman named Matthew Webb. Webb taught himself to swim at the age of 9, and many years later, while in the Cunard Mail Service, dramatically put his swimming ability to use. On April 22, 1873, Webb sailed from New York on the steamship *Russia*. Soon afterward the boat was overtaken by a violent storm with gale force winds whipping the sea into towering 8-foot waves. Suddenly, as the huge boat was tossed about like a cork, a seaman fell from the rigging into the churning 40°F.

(4.4°C.) ocean below. Instinctively Webb dove overboard to rescue his shipmate, but the steamer stayed on course leaving them hopelessly behind. Fortunately, someone had witnessed the episode and immediately reported it. The huge ship turned around and a rescue boat was lowered to search for the men. One hour passed by before Webb was finally spotted in the dark, stormy ocean. The other man was never found.

Matthew Webb, in addition to earning several Royal Humane Society medals for his actions, became inspired by his swim in mid-ocean. He believed that he now had the ability to conquer the English Channel. Realizing that this would require money, he first planned an 18-mile swim in the Thames River. He bet 10 pounds sterling on himself at two-to-one odds and then went on to complete the unprecedented swim in a mere 5 hours. After the race, he collected the money and instead of collapsing in a hotel or hospital, he simply went out to dinner—to everyone's astonishment! What they did not know was that the powerful current had carried Webb most of the distance.

His stunt earned him the admiration of an English newspaperman, Frank Buckland, who offered to sponsor Webb in his attempt to cross the Channel. Webb began training for the brutal swim immediately and found that his 204-pound body could tolerate the cold water temperatures which usually ranged from the high 50's to low 60's F. (14° to 16°C.). His young age (27) also was a great asset for such a strenuous feat.

Buckland's newspaper, *Land and Water*, covered Webb's training expenses and offered 50 pounds sterling for a successful Channel crossing. The paper gave him the much-needed publicity, and the financial offerings grew.

The greatest question facing Webb was what course to follow. He could time his departure to coincide with the flood tide but then eventually he would be carried parallel to the shoreline. Since he was starting from Dover, this plan of attack would risk causing him to swim farther since he might not land at Cape Gris-Nez, the point closest to England. Little was known at that time about the effects of the strong tidal currents. Webb decided to aim for one point at all times rather than ride the currents. By following this route, the tidal currents would cancel each other out.

It was not until the Channel races of the 1950's that Webb's decision was proved to be correct. Once a swimmer is 2 to 3 miles from shore, the tidal currents are never directly against him but are at an angle which allow him to swim across the flow. These currents, however, can affect an approach or departure near a bay or estuary. Webb made a poor choice in going from England to France, however, since it was later discovered that the reverse route is much easier.

On August 12, 1875, Webb greased his body with porpoise oil for insulation and set out at 5 p.m. for Calais. He did not wear goggles and had the boat which accompanied him stocked with brandy, coffee, soup, and cod-liver oil. This poor choice of food later caused seasickness. Since in those days the crawl stroke was unknown to swimmers, Webb used the conventional side-stroke and breast-stroke. He swam well for the first hour but was carried by the currents up the Channel to the northeast. By 10 p.m. the wind came up and 4-foot waves developed. By 11:45 p.m. Webb had been carried way off course, and a storm was brewing. Although still swimming well, he abandoned his first attempt at this point.

This first swim may have been another stunt to arouse interest and raise money, since his failure brought in much more financing to support a second try. Twelve days later when Webb made his next attempt, six London newspapers were present. After nervously greasing up under a clear, sunny sky, he dove into a calm ocean at 12:56 p.m. and swam well for the first few hours. By 4 p.m. the ebb tide had helped him to cover 5½ miles, and the flood tide had begun. Webb received his first food at this time and then continued at a reduced pace since he was being carried up the Channel to the east. At 6:15 p.m. a *Land and Water* reporter dove into the bitter-cold water and swam with Webb for 10 minutes to boost his morale.

An hour passed, and the sky grew dark, making the sea appear black and eerie. Suddenly Webb screamed and clutched at his leg. He had been stung by a jellyfish. To try to combat the growing nausea sweeping over him, he gulped down some brandy. Remembering how some swimmers have died from the stings of the deadly man-of-war, Webb swam completely around the area.

The tidal current reversed itself, and Webb began to make excellent time. A crowd of spectators on a paddle steamer passed by and cheered, lifting the swimmer's spirits. The euphoria was short-lived, however, for by 2 a.m. Webb felt exhausted and depressed. By 3 a.m. he was only 4 miles from France but had been in the water for 14 hours. He worried that the tide would change before he got close enough to shore. If it did, he would be pulled mercilessly away from land.

Early morning, when distance swimmers are tired and surrounded by darkness, is the most trying time of all. Many give up at this point, and Webb seriously considered it. In the next hour he swam only one mile, and then the tide shifted once again, pulling him parallel to the coastline and stopping all progress. When the sun rose at 6:30 a.m., the wind gathered force while the choppy sea carried him away from his destination, Cape Gris-Nez, and toward Calais. By 9 a.m. the escort boats were being drenched by waves. Webb's assistants talked of his quitting, but he struggled onward. Between 4 a.m. and 10 a.m. he was carried for 13 miles parallel to the shoreline. Only a mile and a half from land, waves were washing over the exhausted swimmer. His boat took up a position on his windward side to break the brutal force of the waves, until finally the tidal currents weakened, allowing Webb to draw within a half mile of shore. However, he was then barely swimming at all so an assistant dove in and swam with him for encouragement.

Hundreds of spectators cheered him on as he groggily crawled onto the beach. Unable to walk, he was carried ashore by several of them amidst tears and smiles. Webb was rushed to a nearby hotel and examined by a doctor. After surviving the cold water for 21 hours 45 minutes, his vital signs were completely normal. In covering 21 miles, he actually swam 50, and his feat was not repeated until 36 years later! More than 70 attempts were made during that time.

Webb collected $20,000 that year and an

Having braved and conquered the English Channel, received medals for a heroic mid-ocean attempt to rescue a man overboard, 35-year-old Matthew Webb went to a watery grave a short distance above Niagara Falls.

additional $25,000 from the Prince of Wales. After making public appearances, and so forth, in England, he eventually moved to the United States. In 1883, he was down to a $15,000 bank account and decided to try another money-making feat. This attempt was to be a crossing of the Niagara River above the falls.

This ill-fated swim lasted only 15 minutes. Webb apparently struck a whirlpool and was dragged under the churning water. His body was recovered down-river at Lewiston where it was later buried. Webb was only 35 years old when he died.

Gertrude Ederle

By the 1920's the Channel had been conquered several times, and swimming was finally being approached scientifically. Swimming pools were being built to help young athletes train for the Olympics, and distance swimming was gaining popularity.

In 1926 the name Gertrude "Trudy" Ederle

At the tender age of 14, Trudy Ederle was already famous for having trounced a field of 50 great swimmers in a race in New York Bay.

became a folk heroine overnight. Having learned to swim at an early age, she joined the Women's Swimming Association. At 14 she made her mark in the swimming world by beating 50 world-famous competitors in a 3-mile race in New York Bay. Impressed with this showing, her club funded her trip to England for an attempt in the Channel. In her first venture, however, the weather turned foul and forced a defeat.

In 1926, the *Chicago Tribune* and the *New York News* Syndicate sponsored another trip for the amiable teenager. Much publicity was showered on her as she spent weeks training in the frigid seas off Cape Gris-Nez.

Finally, on August 6, the weather mercifully allowed Trudy to begin her historic crossing. Newsmen and photographers in chartered boats witnessed a smooth, fast start from the French shoreline at dawn. Trudy swam well until late afternoon when a sudden squall moved into the Channel. As she bobbed up and down among the mountainous waves, her trainer pleaded with her to quit. She ignored his shouts and by 6:30 p.m. could see the White Cliffs of Dover.

During the final two hours of the swim, thousands of admirers gathered on the shoreline, ablaze with hundreds of flares to guide the teenager in. Car horns blared and tugboat sirens wailed as Trudy, smiling and laughing, strode ashore unaided at 9:40 p.m.

Her unprecedented feat in a record-breaking time of 14 hours 31 minutes brought out nearly 2 million Americans to welcome her home to New York. Only a few weeks later Mrs. Mille Carde Corson, a mother of two, became the second woman in history to cross the Channel.

became a household word as the 18-year-old American became the first woman in history to successfully swim the English Channel. She also established a new record for the fastest time.

The daughter of a German immigrant who ran a New York delicatessen, lovable Trudy

Ted May's Final Swim

In his home town of Dartford, England, Ted May was regarded as a powerful swimmer. As a teenager he swam the lower Thames River to visit his girl friend, Florence, and enjoyed frightening her by crossing the river on stormy nights or diving beneath the surface and staying under for long periods. He took great pride in his swimming ability and boasted that one day he would swim to France.

Ted's marriage to Florence forced his swimming ambitions aside for many years. At the age of 44, however, Ted decided it was time to enter the Butlin Channel Race and fulfil his childhood goal. He was refused entry into the 1954 race, however, for medical reasons. Convinced that it was his last chance, he decided to swim the English Channel alone.

In September, the 6-foot-2-inch, 240-pound steelworker waded into the surf off Cape Gris-Nez, towing an inner tube filled with supplies behind him. It contained a compass, two bottles of rum, sliced chicken, sugar, and biscuits to help him through a long ordeal. After 5 hours Ted was ravenous, but the chicken and biscuits were already gone. He gulped down some rum and continued on toward the White Cliffs of Dover. The skies were clear, and his spirits high until suddenly foul weather moved over the Channel. The skies blackened, and the rain poured down in blinding torrents.

Frightened and bewildered, the lone Englishman decided to turn around and head back to France. Fighting for his life, he swam for 2 hours until he spotted a ship on the horizon. The Norwegian freighter miraculously pulled alongside the swimmer and attempted to rescue him from the rough sea. Since the ocean was too choppy to launch a lifeboat the crew tied a rope around the exhausted figure and hauled him aboard. Undaunted and insisting that he had merely hit a bad spot, Ted May vowed to try again in a few weeks.

True to his word, Ted kissed his wife and children good-bye 2 weeks later and boarded a boat headed for Calais. Appalled that he was going to try again, the French police attempted to stop him by revoking his passport. The determined swimmer, however, again entered the chilly sea off Cape Gris-Nez on September 19, 1954. This time he was greased and goggled, wore a luminous wrist compass, and again towed a raft filled with supplies.

After 12 hours at sea, the weather turned violent as it so often does in the Channel. At the end of 15 hours a full gale was blowing and the sea had become churning white water. Suddenly the tanker, *San Vito*, radioed, "Man in sea near Goodwin Sands!" Crew members had miraculously spotted the lone man frantically waving his arms while being tossed mercilessly about in the violent sea. The chief officer threw in a lifebelt, but it fell short by 20 feet. By the time the huge ship turned back toward the man 8 minutes later, he was nowhere to be seen. Lifeboats, warships, air-sea rescue planes, and helicopters set out immediately into the stormy night. The sky exploded with parachute flares, but no sign of the swimmer was found.

The following morning Florence waited faithfully for her husband on Dover Sands. Knowing that storms had never beaten him before, she refused to give up hope. After 32 hours, however, the R.A.F. planes and boats abandoned the fruitless search. At the end of the month a corpse with a compass strapped to a wrist was washed ashore in Holland.

Antonio Abertondo

The early 1950's were profitable years for professional swimmers. The best collected over $100,000 per year by swimming the international circuit. Antonio Abertondo, however, was too slow for such competition. In fact the 5-foot-4-inch, 225-pound Argentinean was considered to be the world's worst swimmer since he had no form, rhythm, or speed. What Abertondo did have was staying power.

"The world's worst swimmer," 42-year-old Antonio Abertondo, here waves from the water a half mile off the English coast as he nears the end of his unprecedented round-trip swim of the English Channel on September 22, 1961.

Tony, the son of a Buenos Aires postman, taught himself to swim at the age of 11. He grew up only a few blocks from where South America's La Plata River opens into a 30- to 60-mile-wide mouth. This is where he first learned to swim and where he developed an interest in distance events.

He later became famous for his endurance after completing a number of swims over 60 hours in length including one which lasted for 4 days non-stop in the Paraná River. He twice completed 30-hour swims across the La Plata River from Uruguay to Argentina, a distance of more than 50 miles. The La Plata is a warm, dependable river, however, unlike the English Channel which has been known to carry helpless swimmers into the North Sea.

One year an enthusiastic English newspaperman, Sam Rockett, suggested that Tony attempt a two-way crossing of the Channel. Since Abertondo was not fast enough to set speed records in the Channel, he decided that this was a good alternative. No one had ever

survived more than $27\frac{1}{2}$ hours in the Channel, but he was determined that he could. After training 8 hours a day through 1960 into the spring of 1961, Tony was ready for the swim.

Weather conditions were poor, however, and the swim was postponed until September. In the meantime, Ted Erikson set a new world record for open-water swimming by going 44 miles across Lake Michigan. (See page 79.) When Tony finally made his first attempt in September, the weather in the Channel again turned bad, forcing the frustrated swimmer out of the water after 15 hours.

Only two weeks later Abertondo again entered the chilling seas off Dover on a cloudy, cold day. He knew he would have to complete the first leg of the round trip within 16 hours in order to have favorable tides off the coast of France. Tony took almost 19 hours, however, landing on a deserted French shore in the early morning. Only one photographer and one journalist greeted the exhausted swimmer, providing little encouragement for his return journey. Within 4 minutes, Abertondo quickly downed a hot drink, regreased, and slipped back into the sea.

During the afternoon the skies cleared, and Tony swam well. By 6 p.m. that evening, however, the drama began to grow tense. Tony was failing fast and could not understand why the cliffs directly ahead were not getting any closer. The shriveled-up figure with swollen tongue, cracked lips, and raspy voice looked and sounded like a dying man. He continually begged his crew, "How far?"

Gradually Abertondo's eyes grew more swollen and bloodshot until all he could see were hallucinations. Tony accused the crew of sabotaging him by leading him in circles and salting his drinking water. Suddenly, he shouted at his coach, "Those posts! Why must I swim through those posts!" Then he asked, "What are these cursed dogs doing in the water? Who put them there?"

His bewildered, sympathetic trainer began thrashing at the water with an oar until Abertondo was convinced that the dogs had been chased away. The retired, veteran swimmer, Sam Rockett, dove in and swam next to Tony for the last mile until they reached the bottom of the 300-foot-high cliffs. Not only was there no crowd to greet the victorious swimmer, there was no access to the shore where they landed. Tony merely stumbled a few steps, slumped exhausted and incoherent on a rock, and cried. After 43 hours 5 minutes, Antonio Abertondo became the first man in history to complete a double-crossing of the English Channel. Tony was 42 years old at the time.

Ted Erikson

A 37-year-old chemist from Chicago, Illinois, Ted Erikson also made his mark on the English Channel by completing a double crossing in September, 1965. He established a new world record in that swim, but he required three attempts before becoming successful. In his first

two tries, Ted used a computerized course which had been worked out at the Illinois Institute of Technology's Research Center. The program was designed to choose the route which would use the ever-changing tides to his advantage. The results were that he had to change his compass heading every hour in order to remain perpendicular to the tidal stream. Unfortunately, the captain of Ted's escort boat was unable to put the computer program's results into practice.

On his third attempt, Ted dumped the computer program and swam the conventional route. Fortunately, the weather was ideal, and the only tangible obstacle was the ever-present jellyfish. Erikson completed his first lap from England to France in 14 hours 15 minutes. His

Ensconsed in his escort boat, triumphant Ted Erikson has just completed the second double crossing of the Channel in history. Only a short time before, Ted had hallucinated that the escort boat was a rose bush!

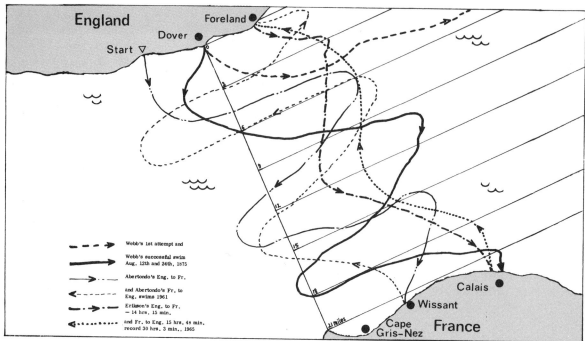

England

Foreland

Dover

Start ▽

Webb's 1st attempt and
Webb's successful swim
Aug. 12th and 24th, 1875
Abertondo's Eng. to Fr.
and Abertondo's Fr. to
Eng. swims 1961
Erikson's Eng. to Fr.
— 14 hrs. 15 min.
and Fr. to Eng. 15 hrs. 48 min.
record 30 hrs. 3 min., 1965

Calais

Wissant

Cape
Gris-Nez   France

Major Channel swims.

return trip went well until the last few miles when he suddenly began hallucinating. The exhausted swimmer saw himself plodding through roses while the escort boat turned into a rose bush. The amazing athlete simply closed his eyes and continued on, reaching the finish with a round trip time of 30 hours 3 minutes, the fastest time for a double crossing up to that time.

Ted Erikson's son, Jon, almost 10 years later in August, 1975, was the one who beat his father's record for the two-way swim—by 3 minutes!

Other Channel Swims

Over the years many dramatic stories unfurled in the Channel. In one swim, the Pakistani, Brojan Das, was almost defeated within 10 yards of shore. After an exhausting 15-hour swim he reached the surf line barely

able to go on. Suddenly, a powerful wave tossed him like a piece of driftwood onto a large flat rock. The incoherent swimmer was unable to move, and his crew was not allowed to touch him. To make matters worse, the incident occurred during an international cross-Channel race, and he was in first place. Fortunately, another giant wave picked him up and swept him into the cliffs to victory.

*   *   *

The first Channel race took place in 1950 with 24 top swimmers competing from all over the world. The most determined among them must have been Fahmy Attallah who was still swimming after 26 hours. Within 300 yards of shore he battled the merciless current for more than an hour. He barely moved at all and frequently rested on his back. As time went on, he grew more dazed and exhausted, bordering on unconsciousness. Suddenly, Attallah tried frantically to sprint, but reversed his direction and headed back toward France. Officials ordered his crew to touch him so that he would be disqualified. After 27 hours 30 minutes in the churning sea, Attallah, crying, "I could have made it," was pulled from the water short of his goal.

*   *   *

The longest successful crossing in history was by an American, Henry Sullivan. In 1923, Henry struggled for 26 hours 50 minutes before completing the swim.

*   *   *

The climax of all the Channel crossings occurred one year when a group of Americans sent over Pierre, a trained seal, to swim between France and England. Pierre set the fastest time to date: 5 hours, compared to the official Channel Swimming Association record of 8 hours 56 minutes set by Wendy Brooks on August 31, 1976.

*   *   *

The first recorded drowning occurred on September 29, 1926, when a young Spaniard, Luis Rodriguez Delara, attempted to swim the Channel without an escort boat or any food. His body was washed ashore at Boulogne.

*   *   *

In 1962, deciding that Channel swimming had become too commonplace, an American swam from Cape Gris-Nez to Pegwell Bay entirely under water with scuba. Fred Baldassare, age 38, following a fishing boat for navigation, swam 9 feet below the surface for 18 hours 1 minute. Scuba divers supplied him with fresh tanks of air every so often. Baldassare spent his life savings of $35,000 preparing for the epic swim and then convinced his wife to try also. She attempted the same stunt twice but failed. They were divorced soon afterward.

*   *   *

One would think that by 1974 the era of Channel swimming would have been over. Not so, however, for on one August day alone there were 20 swimmers fighting the sea between England and France, and 11 more impatiently waiting at Dover for an official Channel pilot. The coast guard had their hands full patrolling the world's busiest shipping lane cluttered with a logjam of swimmers.

Among those attempting to make a name for themselves was 19-year-old Sandra Keshka. Sandra, a member of the "men's" swimming team at San Diego State College, was trying for a one-way record that August day. After consulting the tide tables and weather conditions, she decided to attempt the France-to-England route.

At 3:22 a.m. on the last ebb of the tide, she waded into the sea off Normandy Beach and headed west. She soon would catch the flood tide which would carry her up toward St. Margaret's Bay on the English side. At the same time a 47-year-old Australian, Desmond Renford, was battling the currents while trying to reach the French shore. Renford had crossed the Channel four times previously and on three of these occasions had attempted a double crossing.

On this particular day, he was trying to break the record two-way crossing time of 30 hours 3 minutes set in 1965 by Ted Erikson. Each time previously the powerful tidal currents and wind had defeated Renford on the second leg. In 1972, he came within 6 miles of England on the return trip when suddenly a 25-mile-per-hour wind combined with a 4.7 knot ebb tide to carry him helplessly 35 miles up the Channel. The persistent Australian, however, did not give in until he found himself off the Belgian coast.

Sandra was accompanied on her attempt by her coach, the great American Channel swimmer of the 1950's, Florence Chadwick (see page 92). The two athletes waited several weeks before this swim, but Chadwick took the delay in stride, having once waited for 4 months in Dover for a change in weather. Florence was excited about Sandra's swim since she felt the youngster was faster than she had ever been and faster than Lynne Cox, who held the unofficial world record.

Also in the water that August day were several relay teams. One consisted of six jovial, husky policemen from Long Island, all members of the Eastern Marathon Swimming Association of Glen Cove. The entire team spent the previous evening in the police club bar, bragging that they would swim three ways: France to England, England to France, and back again. They were already known for their 150-mile swim from Montauk Point on Long Island to Sheepshead Bay off Brooklyn. That relay set an unofficial world record in 108 hours 25 minutes. Another team, the Texas Volunteers, was captained by Tom Hetzel who had made six successful Channel crossings.

This motley assortment of swimmers ended up in the English Channel on the same day due to an unusual combination of favorable neap tides, relatively warm (62°F. or 16.6°C.) water, and little wind. When the R.A.F. reported that the next blow would not start for 12 hours, everyone took off. The Texas Volunteers, the Nassau County cops, and Des Renford plunged in during mid-evening while Sandra Keshka, with Florence Chadwick in the escort boat, left in the early morning.

Sandra swam with difficulty at first since the lights on her escort boat blinded her, causing her to veer away. By mid-Channel she was swimming well with a steady 85 strokes per minute, periodically stopping for her feeding of broth and glucose tablets.

At 9 a.m. whitecaps began cropping up and the pilot decided to head well up the Channel so that near the end of the swim Sandra could be carried back easily into St. Margaret's Bay. Over the radio the crew heard that Renford had reached France, but was badly battered by the violent waves. It had taken him $4\frac{1}{2}$ hours to swim the last 2 miles. He then headed back toward England for a double crossing but was

Sandra Keshka, a member of the "men's" swimming team at San Diego State College, receives a congratulatory hug and kiss from her coach Florence Chadwick after successfully crossing the English Channel on August 15, 1974.

forced to quit 8 miles off the English coast. Renford lasted for 22 hours 52 minutes before being defeated.

At the end of 9 hours of swimming, Florence reluctantly told Sandra that she did not have a chance to break the record. The sea had grown wild and a gale force wind continually blew her off course. Sandra bravely continued on toward the White Cliffs of Dover and finally landed east of St. Margaret's Bay. Her time of 10 hours 30 minutes was excellent considering the foul weather and, surprisingly, was only 1 hour longer than Cox's record time.

No one heard anything from the New York cops, apparently fogbound off the coast of France. All Thursday morning people wondered if they were all right. Finally, the amiable, none-too-serious group was spotted drinking champagne in the Holiday Inn pool in Dover. When someone innocently asked about their three-way swim, they gleefully tossed him in the pool along with the hotel barman, and the receptionist.

17. The Wrigley Catalina Island Swim

Santa Catalina, one of the Channel Islands, is located 22 miles off the coast south of Los Angeles. The largest prize ever offered for a marathon swim up until 1927 was awarded in the Wrigley Swim to that island in that year.

In 1919, Philip K. Wrigley, the chewing gum magnate, had bought Catalina and converted the barren island into a quaint resort area. The island became a popular tourist attraction during the summer months with 30,000 visitors flocking to it each year. During the winter, however, Catalina and its 1,500 year-round inhabitants suffered financially.

Wrigley, seeking publicity for his investment, decided to promote a swimming race from Catalina across the San Pedro Channel to Point Vincente, near Long Beach. He set the date for January 20, 1927. The first athlete to reach the lighthouse located there would win $25,000. The first woman to finish would walk away with $15,000.

The Wrigley Catalina Island Swim was promoted as being more difficult than swimming the English Channel since the Channel was only 21 miles across whereas the Catalina Swim would be 22 miles. Immediately prior to the race, however, the starting point was moved from the harbor to the isthmus of Catalina, making the new distance only 18.5 miles. It is possible that the promoters feared no one would complete the longer course.

One entrant in the Catalina Swim was a 17-year-old Canadian named George Young. Although he had won many Canadian medals, he was broke and had trouble financing the 2,500-mile trip to the race. Using his meager earnings from a part-time job, he and a friend bought a motorcycle and sidecar to make the journey to southern California. The two boys intended to arrive in Los Angeles by Christmas so that Young would have three weeks to train for the big event.

Their ill-fated trip was besieged with problems. The motorcycle continually broke down, but, undaunted, the two companions got jobs along the way to earn money for repairs. Young trained wherever he could find swimming pools or water, but often was unable to locate either. Fortunately, in Little Rock, Arkansas, they met a sympathetic newlywed couple who offered to drive them to Los Angeles.

As soon as he arrived, Young began a regular training program, swimming 3 to 5 miles each day. One day he met an enterprising stranger who offered to accompany Young during the race in a boat in order to feed him. He also was willing to pay Young's expenses for the three weeks prior to the race while the swimmer trained. As Young's "manager" he would receive 40 per cent of the prize money and the same percentage of any money George earned from the race during the following year. The naive 17-year-old agreed, and the stranger sent off a contract to Young's mother to sign.

A motley mob of over 100 hopefuls wearing everything from nothing to long johns greased up and swarmed into the bone-chilling San Pedro Channel at Catalina Island in California on January 20, 1927. This was the start of the Wrigley Catalina to Point Vincente swim, the brainchild of chewing-gum entrepreneur Philip K. Wrigley.

On January 15, a total of 145 entrants arrived at the island for the start of the race. Some had already proven themselves in the English Channel, and many others held amateur records. The favorite was Norman "Big Moose" Ross, a 250-pound national and world record holder from the Illinois Athletic Club in Chicago. Ross appealed greatly to the spectators due to his glib tongue, which later earned him a position as a Chicago radio announcer. Unlike other racers the well-padded Ross refused to use grease as protection from the bitter cold and did not even wear a a swim suit, preferring to race nude instead.

The extremely cold water temperatures that winter day on January 20, however, shocked everyone, and 43 contestants dropped out during the first few hours before the start. The temperatures in the San Pedro Channel ranged from 54° to 65°F. (12° to 18.3°C.), putting the thinner athletes at a severe disadvantage. Unlike Ross, one swimmer even wore long underwear coated with grease.

While newsmen and tourists alike converged on Catalina's isthmus, the atmosphere grew carnival-like with endless ceremonies and picture-taking. At 11:21 a.m. the starting gun was fired and a roar went up from the motley crowd. An odd assortment of hopefuls dove in and began sprinting the first leg of the punishing 18.5-mile course. Others stood back and waited for the water to clear before plunging in. After a few minutes a total of 102 contestants, including a legless boy that someone threw in, clogged the chilly waters.

After 3 minutes George Young took the lead with Ross fighting to keep up with him. Upon clearing the harbor, the Canadian's "coach" changed his compass heading and aimed for a point north of the lighthouse. He wrongly believed that during the final stages of the race when the boy would surely be exhausted, he could merely ride downstream to the finish line.

As in the English Channel crossings, it was later proved that a constant heading in the San Pedro Channel Swim was fastest. Fortunately for Young, Ross' boat followed him instead of taking the shorter route that many others took.

During the first hour the painfully cold water took its toll and forced 30 more swimmers to quit. Ross and Young pulled ahead of the pack and, after 2 hours, Young led his opponent by a mere 150 yards. Every time Ross sprinted to catch up, Young sprinted even farther in front.

Seven miles from shore George encountered a common obstacle to open-water swimmers— an oil slick. He worked his way through it and afterward took his first break, drinking two cups of hot chocolate. Many swimmers gave up by this point, and by 5 p.m. a woman named Lottie Schoemmel, who held the world record for swimming around Manhattan Island, was pulled into her escort boat. Her left knee was so swollen that she later was hospitalized for three days.

By 8 p.m. only 20 of the original 102 contestants stroked onward. These few survivors, having suffered through winter cold temperatures for 8½ hours, were discovering that the San Pedro Channel Swim was infinitely more trying than the English Channel crossing because of the incapacitating temperatures. Otherwise, conditions were perfect—the sea was flat with waves never exceeding a foot in height.

Young, seemingly impervious to the cold, stretched his lead over Ross to 1½ miles by 9 p.m. By midnight, thousands of headlights from cars parked atop Point Vincente, combined with the lighthouse beacon, led the swimmers toward shore. Ross, realizing he would probably lose, swore at his crew but continued on. By 2:30 a.m. Young could hear loudspeakers and car horns but suddenly ran into a dense forest of kelp. In spite of the long, vine-like plants entangling his legs and arms, he made his way through it toward shore.

Meanwhile, Ross was told that his opponent would capture first place in less than half an hour. Exhausted and disgusted with being beaten by a 17-year-old, the great swimmer climbed into his escort boat and forfeited second place.

While hundreds of boats focused searchlights on George to guide him in, the judges waded into the bitter cold waters to greet him and help him ashore. He finished before a crowd of 15,000 at 3:06 a.m. after covering a torturous 27 miles in 15 hours 45 minutes! The poor navigation wasted an extra 7 miles but fortunately most of the others suffered through similar problems. As a blanket was thrown around him, George was awarded the $25,000 first prize and an additional $1,000 from the owners of the property on which he landed. As the crowd cheered jubilantly, Young was driven off to the California Yacht Club to be greeted by wealthy admirers. From there he was escorted to a Long Beach hospital for a well-deserved rest. His doctor pronounced him to be fine, having lost only 5 pounds during his exhausting ordeal.

Margaret Hauser and Martha Stager each left the water around 6 a.m. with only a mile to go. Hauser had endured the painful water for 19 hours 26 minutes while Stager lasted for 19 hours 6 minutes. Wrigley rewarded each of the women with $2,500.

"The father of marathon swimming" was a boy of 17. George Young, after winning the Catalina swim, was lionized by fans and promoters alike, but it didn't last. Four years later, he was all but forgotten.

George Young gained instant world-wide recognition and was besieged by promoters within a few days of the race. His manager took 40 per cent of the prize money, signed George up for five nights in a Hollywood theatre for $1,000, and obtained screen tests for him. George, having collected the largest prize for a marathon swim up until that date and being the first person to swim the San Pedro Channel, became known as the father of marathon swimming.

Wrigley reaped such profits from the Catalina Swim that he immediately planned another professional swim (as we will see in the next chapter) for later that year at the Canadian National Exhibition in Toronto, Canada. An unprecedented first place prize of $30,000 was to be offered for the 21-mile swim. Young entered, but was defeated by the 48°F. (9°C.) water temperature after a painful 4 hours. The following year's race was ill-fated since no swimmer was able to stand the bitter cold long enough to complete the race.

George Young, however, did win the C.N.E. race in 1931, but his career went downhill from there. He attempted a comeback at the age of 36, but was unsuccessful. He died in 1972.

When Wrigley died, he was buried on Santa Catalina Island in a mausoleum. In later years the Catalina Swim did not gain much attention and even when Greta Andersen successfully completed a double crossing (see page 97), the public showed little interest.

18. The Canadian National Exhibition Swim

Reflecting on the success of the Catalina Swim, Wrigley planned a similar promotional stunt to broaden his Canadian market. The Canadian National Exhibition, held in August and September each year, annually attracted thousands of spectators. Wrigley presented the officials of the C.N.E. with a grandiose plan for an annual professional swim starting in 1927, the winner of which would be crowned world champion. He promised $50,000 in prizes and expenses.

The Canadians liked the idea and set August 30, 1927, as the date for the first race. The winner would collect $30,000, an unprecedented prize in the world of marathon swimming. The second place award would be $7,500, third $2,500, fourth $1,000, and fifth and sixth $500 each. The first woman to finish would win an additional $5,000 over any original prizes. The second woman to finish would collect $2,500, and the third $500.

A unique 21-mile triangular course was laid out in Lake Ontario with the last mile running in front of the spectator seating area. Many of the swimmers who had competed in the Catalina Swim earlier that year were entered, including George Young, Norman Ross, and Lottie Schoemmel.

The wind had blown all week prior to the race and caused the water temperature to drop to a chilling 51°F. (10.5°C.). As the starting gun fired, the swimmers dove in and set a fast early pace. Young led slightly but was unable to put a significant distance between himself and the others. The cold appeared to affect him this time, and he faltered visibly after only 4 miles. At this point a German swimmer, Ernst Vierkoetter, began to close the gap. At the 5-mile point George found Ernst alongside him, and as the German eventually took over the lead, Young gave up and dejectedly climbed into his escort boat.

At the end of 8 torturous hours of swimming, only 12 athletes remained in the water. Ethel Hertle and Lottie Schoemmel of New York were among them. A raucous crowd of 35,000 began to gather near the finish line. In spite of the water temperature dropping several more degrees, Ernst continued on, stretching his lead to over 2 miles. Finally, at 8:15 p.m. he climbed out of the lake to collect the unprecedented $30,000 first prize. Vierkoetter had completed the chilly 21 miles in 11 hours 45 minutes.

The second place winner, a Frenchman named Georges Michel, was a full 5 hours behind the German and was near collapse at the finish. Many others had left the water throughout the race, because they could not tolerate the cold water temperature.

In 1928, the officials shortened the event to 15 miles so that the spectators would still be there when the swimmers finished. Another major change was that the women were to compete in a separate 10-mile race. Prizes totaling $50,000 again were offered to the 250 competitors who came from all over the world.

On the day of the race the water temperatures in the unpredictable Lake Ontario ranged from 44° to 46°F. (6.6° to 7.7°C.). Only 199 athletes ventured to the starting line and a few minutes after the gun was fired, the first swimmer quit. A demoralized group of 25 others emerged within the next 15 minutes. Ross lasted for 2 hours 27 minutes, but not being among the leaders, he too got out of the frigid lake. A total of 85 per cent of the starters had given up by this early point in the race.

George Young for the second year was forced out by the cold after having lasted for 3 hours 50 minutes. Ernst Vierkoetter pulled in front and held a 2-mile lead over the Frenchman, Georges Michel. At the end of 7 hours, only three determined men remained in the unbearably cold water. They were battling the elements rather than each other.

The third man, an American named Louis Mathias, was dragged onto his escort boat after becoming incoherent. At 4 p.m. the German stopped to talk to his assistants for he held a 3-mile lead over the Frenchman, but was numb from the cold. He had suffered for 11¼ hours but had less than 3 miles to go. After debating the issue for 10 desperate minutes, he pulled himself onto his escort boat and disqualified himself.

The courageous Georges Michel struggled on alone. He quickened his pace after learning that Ernst had given up, but then reluctantly slowed down again. He eventually passed the location where Ernst had left the water but could only go about an eighth of a mile farther. He lasted 3 hours 30 minutes longer than the German, but was finally pulled from the water in a semi-conscious state. By swimming slightly farther than his opponent, Georges Michel collected half of the prize money.

The annual Canadian National Exhibition gained much publicity from this swim and continually attracted great professional swimmers from all over the world. This devastating race, however, became known as a destroyer of reputations, particularly in the case of Norman

Ross. In spite of holding every amateur world record in short distances, Ross never won a professional race in his career. Every year he returned to the Canadian Nationals to regain his former glory, and every year he failed.

The race was not always as painful as in 1928 and as the water temperatures rose, the winning times fell radically. "The Flying Dutchman," Herman Willemse (see page 78), set a record time in 1962 of 6 hours 38 minutes. Lake Ontario was a tepid 73°F. (22.7°C.) on that day.

For the 36 years following the ill-fated 1928 swim, the officials tested courses varying from 5 to 32 miles in length with the 15-mile race becoming the most popular. No events were held from 1938 to 1946 due to World War II, but the postwar era spawned the biggest money winner in the history of swimming.

The amiable Cliff Lumsden from Toronto entered the 1947 Canadian National at the tender age of 16 and beat many of the world's best swimmers by placing sixth. The following year he came in third, and the next year at the age of 18 Lumsden won the event. Cliff dominated the Canadian Nationals during the next few years by collecting the $6,000 first place prize in more races than any other swimmer.

In 1954 Marilyn Bell (then 16 years old) made a historic crossing of Lake Ontario, becoming the first athlete to do so. (See page 101.) The following year the C.N.E. officials decided to capitalize on her publicity by staging a cross-lake swim from Niagara to Toronto. Unfortunately, fickle Mother Nature intervened once again, forcing the course to be reduced to a 32-mile triangular one.

Cliff, adapting easily to the new distance, completed the event in 19 hours 48 minutes, and collected the $15,000 first prize. This was only a small fraction of what he eventually netted from the race since Cliff also collected $1 per stroke for each stroke taken during the final five miles. Advertisers and promoters gave him a new home and an assortment of

The Canadian, Cliff Lumsden, touches the finish line to win the Canadian National Exhibition marathon in 1953. After his first win at the age of 18, he all but took over the event for the next few years—and the $6,000 first prize money.

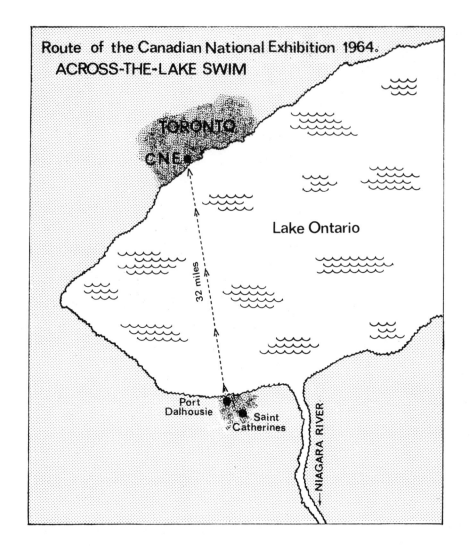

Route of the Canadian National Exhibition 1964.
ACROSS-THE-LAKE SWIM

TORONTO
CNE

Lake Ontario

32 miles

Port Dalhousie

Saint Catherines

NIAGARA RIVER

Route of the 1964 Canadian National Exhibition Swim.

endorsements which eventually multiplied his earnings to $84,000. The crowning glory echoed by all was that it could not have happened to a nicer guy.

The 1964 Lake Ontario Swim may have been the greatest assemblage of professional swimmers in history. Herman Willemse (the Flying Dutchman), Abdel-Latif Abo-Heif (the garrulous, lovable Egyptian), Jim Woods (the record holder for a 1957 crossing of Lake Ontario), John LaCoursiere (winner of the 24-mile Lake St. John Swim and the 1,500-meter amateur champion of Canada), Cliff Lumsden, and

many other world-famous racers were present for the start of the event on August 20.

Two great female swimmers were also present, one being the world's top female competitor, Greta Andersen, and the other an unknown at the time, Judith DeNys. DeNys, a 22-year-old Dutch girl, was entering only her second professional race.

A total of 24 starters were competing for the $7,000 first prize and the $17,500 total prize money. Abo-Heif was favored to win, while Greta Andersen was predicted to place second.

For decades swimmers and trainers alike

have debated what the best pre-race meal should be. The diets of the 5-foot-10-inch, 205-pound Abo-Heif and the 145-pound Judith DeNys are examples of the extremes. While waiting for the 6 p.m. start, Abo-Heif consumed two whole roast chickens, a 12-egg omelet, an entire plate of spaghetti, and several wedges of cheddar cheese. DeNys merely nibbled at tomato sandwiches washed down with weak tea.

As the starting time approached, the anxious swimmers grew tense. Most of them greased their bodies as token protection against the water's chill, while officials issued each contestant bathing caps with fluorescent lights. Although the lake was a mild 72°F. (23°C.) prior to the start of the race six swimmers including Herman Willemse dropped out of the competition entirely. Since Willemse always monitored temperatures carefully, the others should have noted his decision.

When the gun was fired at 6 p.m., 18 starters plunged into the unpredictable Lake Ontario. Abo-Heif, Andersen, Lumsden, DeNys, and LaCoursiere led the pack at the start. After two hours the group had covered over 3½ miles, but the water had already dropped 3°F. The first problem arose at the end of three hours when the Argentinean, Romero Florencio, was forced to tread water due to stomach cramps. A few minutes later Claudia McPherson, who at 16 years of age had been the youngest swimmer ever to cross the English Channel, quit the race due to pulled leg muscles.

By this time DeNys, Andersen, and Abo-Heif held the lead, and LaCoursiere had had to drop out due to cramps. The fluorescent light went out on 42-year-old Charles Grover's cap, forcing him to swim next to his boat to avoid getting lost. By 10 p.m. the water temperature, having dropped to 65°F. (18.3°C.), caused many more athletes to quit the race.

Meanwhile Lumsden and Abo-Heif were becoming irritated with the fast pace that novice Judith DeNys was setting. Even more annoying was her habit of sprinting ahead of the others every 15 minutes. Abo-Heif decided to sprint for a full half-hour to break her and managed to pull a quarter mile ahead. It took DeNys a full hour to catch up with the Egyptian, and it did stop her from sprinting again.

Other swimmers continuously dropped out during the race, and by 1 a.m. the water was a bone-chilling 61°F. (16°C.). At this point blue-faced Cliff Lumsden climbed aboard his escort boat and was quickly wrapped in blankets. This marked only the second time in 18 years of competitive swimming that he had ever given up during a race.

Seemingly impervious to the cold, Abo-Heif and DeNys stroked on side-by-side 15 miles from shore. At 2 a.m. Judith stopped for her hourly tea and glucose feeding served by her mother who was following in a rowboat. Abo-Heif, realizing the mental strength derived from swimming next to a competitor, stopped whenever Judith did. He was continually accused of being a leech, but knew he did not need to sprint in front of his pacer until a few miles from the finish.

At this point Greta Andersen lagged a half mile behind followed by Ken Jensen, George Park, Mohomed Zaitoon, and Mary Lou Whitwell. Charlie Grover plodded along easily and steadily 5 miles behind Abo-Heif and DeNys. For 2 hours the water temperature remained at 59°F. (15°C.), but the swimmers had no idea what was ahead of them. They were becoming cold and exhausted after 10 hours in the lake, and at 4:55 a.m. Mary Lou Whitwell was dragged aboard her boat unconscious. Almost an hour later Greta Andersen cheerfully gave up, deliriously happy that the ordeal was over. She was immediately rushed to an ambulance waiting in Toronto.

At dawn, only Abo-Heif, DeNys, Park, Jensen, and Grover remained in the 55°F. (12.8°C.) water. They swam on through a 1½-foot chop, but at 7:15 a.m. Judith stopped swimming. Abo-Heif encouraged her to keep going but finally left her behind. Later he was surprised to see her alongside him again.

At 8:30 a.m. the Egyptian picked up his pace to 60 strokes per minute. At the end of $14\frac{1}{2}$ torturous hours of swimming, Abo-Heif had a firm grip on first place and only 5 miles to go. Judith, looking even more erratic, began swimming in wide circles. Her mother could not direct her and was horrified to see that her body was turning blue, a symptom of stagnant blood.

At 10 a.m. Mrs. DeNys reluctantly reached over and touched her daughter in order to disqualify her. DeNys was immediately wrapped in blankets and taken to a hospital in Montreal where it took her two days to recover.

Jensen and then Park dropped out of the race.

Now only Abo-Heif was in the lead, but the water was down to 53°F. (11.6°C.). Swimming less than a mile an hour, he passed the $29\frac{1}{2}$-mile point. Suddenly, his handlers saw the great athlete swimming in the wrong direction, not responding to their shouts, and showing no intention of quitting. His crew threw a rope in front of him and as soon as he hit it, they all cheered as if he had crossed the finish line. Abo-Heif hesitated long enough for them to wrap the rope around him and pull him on board. This was a painful moment for everyone since there were only 2 miles to go, and Abo-Heif had never previously quit a race in his life.

It was 12:46 p.m., and the only swimmer still in the water was 42-year-old Charlie Grover. He lasted for two more hours but only reached the 20-mile mark, when the water was still a comparatively balmy 59°F. (15°C.).

The Canadian Nationals received such bad publicity from the swimmers having to be carted off in stretchers that the officials immediately canceled all future races. Prizes were awarded for this final race based on the distance each competitor covered. Abo-Heif collected $4,400, DeNys $2,850, Tom Park $1,250, Grover $950, Andersen $775, Jensen $650, and Zaitoon $450.

Tom Park, already two-time winner of the Atlantic City race, plows through the water in the 1958 event 500 yards in the lead at the halfway mark.

19. Atlantic City Races

In 1954, a marathon came into existence that was designed solely for spectator appeal. The site of the event was Atlantic City, a summer resort area located on the end of Absecon Island on the southern New Jersey coast. Although the island had never been circled by a swimmer previously, it appeared to be possible since it was surrounded by ocean on one side and a narrow strait on the others.

The island has had a colorful history, having been settled by oystermen, whalers, and pirates. By the mid-19th century, shipyards, iron plants, and other types of industry had infiltrated the area. Over the years, commercial and sport fishing became prosperous and popular activities, and then tourism became the leading industry.

In 1870, the first boardwalk was constructed along the edge of the beaches. The hotels and restaurants wanted this to decrease the amount of sand tracked into the buildings. The present boardwalk was built in 1939 and is 4 miles long and 60 feet wide. As more and more tourists were attracted to the beach, the city officials searched for additional unique entertainment.

In 1876, the first annual Easter Parade was staged, and in 1921 the first Miss America Pageant was run. Atlantic City soon became a Mecca for conventioneers and has drawn as many as 160,000 visitors a year.

In 1953, Jim Toomey conjured up the idea of an Atlantic City marathon around the island. Since he was not sure if it was possible, he asked two lifeguards, Ed Solitaire and Ed Stetser, to try it. They in turn commandeered two friends to row the escort boat.

Radio WOND advertised the 26-mile swim which was to start on the morning of August 5, 1953. About 200 newsmen and spectators gathered at the Steel Pier awaiting the start. The swim offered no major obstacles since the water was a warm 76°F. (24.4°C.), and the only currents were on the opposite ends of the island at Absecon Inlet and Great Egg Harbor Inlet. In addition there were about 20 piers built out on the ocean side that would serve to protect the swimmers.

The two lifeguards dove from the Steel Pier and swam about a half mile from shore while heading southwest. They continued on throughout the morning and reached the end of the island and the entrance to the channel by early afternoon. They entered Great Egg Harbor Inlet at slack tide and headed north up the narrow strait. Spectators gathered throughout the day at street ends above the water.

Suddenly, Ed Stetser slowed down about 3 miles into the channel. Solitaire attempted to maintain his pace, but soon both swimmers slacked off drastically. In spite of this the two men did extremely well since their longest

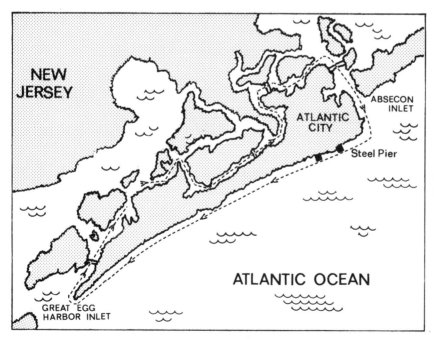

Route of the Atlantic City marathon.

Cliff Lumsden, shown here in the lead in the 1956 race, and Tom Park dominated the swim around Absecon Island for several years—until 1960 when "The Flying Dutchman," Herman Willemse, took over.

previous swim was merely 2½ hours, and they had not trained for this event.

After being in the water for 12 hours, Solitaire inched his way into Absecon Inlet with only 3 miles remaining. Again he had no current to contend with since it was just after high tide, but being exhausted he switched to the breaststroke. The final 3 miles took 2½ hours, and Solitaire finally touched the Steel Pier after 14 hours of steady swimming. One hour later Stetser arrived to find his friend faithfully waiting for him, and the two jubilantly christened what was to become an annual event for years to come.

The following year was the city's centennial celebration so the owner of the Steel Pier,

George A. Hamid, offered $5,000 to the swimmer winning an around-the-island race. More prizes were offered by local businessmen, and a date was set.

Famous swimmers entering that year's race were Cliff Lumsden (who had won the C.N.E. race four times), Tom Park (who had won and placed in several professional races), and Marilyn Bell (who was unknown at that time but was to make the first crossing in history of Lake Ontario a few weeks later). The day of the event was perfect with an ocean temperature of 70°F. (21°C.) and a channel temperature of 82°F. (27.7°C.). A total of 25 starters dove from the Steel Pier and immediately set a fast pace creating an exciting race.

The competitors remained in a pack for the first two hours, until the two Canadians, Tom Park and Cliff Lumsden, pulled out in front. Spectators lining the beaches and the boardwalk watched them cover 5 miles in only two hours. As they reached the inner waterway, they could see thousands of observers cheering them on at the first bridge.

An American, Steve Wozniak, was only a block behind the Canadians and tried valiantly to maintain their $2\frac{1}{2}$-mile-per-hour pace. With a full $2\frac{1}{2}$ miles to go, Park and Lumsden realized that they would have to sprint for one to obtain a solid lead over the other. For the next 25 minutes, one and then the other would pull ahead. Gradually with $1\frac{1}{2}$ miles to go, Lumsden started to fall behind. Within a half mile of the finish, Park stretched his lead to 100 yards and swam as hard as he could. An immense crowd of 15,000 spectators awaited him at the pier. As he reached the finish, he turned to see Lumsden only 250 yards behind. Park had set a record (9 hours 21 minutes 42 seconds) which would not be broken during the next 10 years.

This rivalry between the two Canadians continued for many years in both the C.N.E. and the Atlantic City races. In 1955, Park again won the New Jersey race by coming in ahead of Lumsden by a mere 6 minutes. In 1957, Lumsden reaped a narrow revenge by beating Park by 1/20th of a second, or one stroke! The finish was so close that officials later based such decisions on the moment when the swimmer's head crosses the finish.

In 1960, the nature of the marathon changed drastically. The unassuming Dutch grammar school teacher, Herman Willemse (see page 70), came to Atlantic City with nautical charts and tide tables. Using his brains, he managed to beat the two Canadians by a full 10 minutes. Park and Lumsden settled for a second-place tie. The "Flying Dutchman" went on to win the Atlantic City race every year for the next 4 years.

The officials even tried to make the race harder by running it against the tides. The swimmers again outsmarted them by grabbing onto submerged obstacles to pull themselves along. At one point Greta Andersen and the Dutchman Willemse were left stranded on a pier when a wave dropped out from under them. All the swimmers suffered cut fingers, some even requiring stitches, as they made their way through broken bottles and wire hidden in the channel.

The public grew bored with the race after Willemse won it for the fifth time in 1964. The sponsors were frantic and even wrote the Dutchman asking him what they should do. Herman wrote back that he would agree to come in second if paid $5,000 prior to the race! The promoters offered $3,000, but Willemse refused. On this note, the 1964 Atlantic City race was the last one to be held.

20. Lake Michigan Races

In 1959, Lake Michigan was still virgin territory for marathon swimmers. An enthusiastic young Chicago lifeguard named Joe Griffith decided he would be the first to conquer the lake by swimming $36\frac{3}{4}$ miles from Chicago to Michigan City, Indiana. He faithfully trained for 5 to 10 miles each day, but worried that he would be unable to find an escort boat to accompany him free.

While training one day, Griffith noticed another swimmer attempting to maintain the lifeguard's brisk pace. Later, on the beach the man walked over, introducing himself as Jim Moran. Saying that he was very impressed with Griffith's swimming, he asked why the young athlete was training so hard. The lifeguard explained about his dream of crossing Lake Michigan and his problems with financing an escort boat. The two men talked enthusiastically for hours about the proposed trip, and Moran eventually volunteered his money and services. He could well afford it since at the time he owned the world's largest Ford dealership. An extra bonus was that Moran was familiar to local Chicago residents for his jovial, folksy television commercials, a medium he later used to promote the swim.

Only 6 weeks later in August, 1959, Griffith made his first attempt to cross the vast lake. Moran financed the escort boats, but Joe was forced to quit in a state of exhaustion after covering 23 miles. In spite of his failure, the newspapers loved the story and Moran received much publicity. The congenial businessman offered to sponsor Griffith again the following year and even brought him on television to talk about his training program, and so on. The public became highly interested in what they now called the Jim Moran Swim. By August, newsmen from all over the area were present to cover the entire event. Results were broadcast over the radio every hour, and a great human interest story developed.

Unfortunately, this swim was badly timed for, after a grueling 27 miles, Joe ran directly into a thunderstorm. Visibility dropped to zero, 4-foot waves lashed against the boats, and lightning lit up the turbulent skies. The crews in the four boats escorting the swimmer were unable to keep him in sight and began to fear for their own lives. By 1 a.m. Griffith had been in the water for 17 hours, and the crew was demanding that he give up. After arguing for several minutes, Joe reluctantly pulled himself on board and headed back.

1961 Lake Michigan Race

Although Joe Griffith gave birth to the famous Lake Michigan races, he never came back for another try. Moran awarded the lifeguard $3,600 and was happy with the great amount of publicity he got for his business. So he decided to turn the event into an annual professional race for all qualified swimmers. Moran hired an advertising and public relations firm, escort boats, crew members, and so on, before suddenly realizing that it was costing him tens of thousands of dollars. He was in too far to back out, however, so he set the date of the Lake Michigan challenge for the spring of 1961, and the course to be 36¾ miles from the center of Chicago to Michigan City, Indiana.

Moran received hundreds of applications for the race from high school and college team members, and such, but none from professionals. He decided both to limit the field to 20 swimmers in order to reduce expenses, and also to stage a 10-mile qualifying event in July. In order to be eligible for the much longer spring race, the competitors would have to complete the 10-mile course in 10 hours or less.

On qualifying day only 25 athletes arrived for the start from Chicago's North Side. Of these only six swam to the downtown area in the required time. Dennis Matuch, an 18-year-old Chicago lifeguard, and Ted Erikson, the Chicago chemist, placed first and second, christening the beginning of a long but competitive friendship.

On the day of the Lake Michigan classic, August 21, 1961, officials arrived early near Chicago's McCormick Place to inspect the water conditions. They did not like what they found, since the wind was blowing at 10 miles per hour and 2-foot waves were visible offshore. Moran could only pray that the lake would flatten out, since to postpone it now would hurt financially.

At 7:55 a.m. six anxious swimmers, adrenaline flowing and bodies covered with grease, awaited the starting gun. They were Ted Erikson, Dennis Matuch, sisters Kathryn Simecek, 18, and Cynthia Simecek, 21, Mary Margaret Revel, and Elmer Korbai.

At the start, Dennis took an early lead in spite of the waves breaking over him. The Simecek sisters lagged 25 yards back followed by Korbai, Revel, and Erikson. Revel was the first to quit, lasting only two hours. By noon, water conditions grew from bad to worse with the wind blowing at 15 miles per hour and the waves topping 3 feet.

By 2 p.m. Dennis Matuch disgustedly hauled himself on board his escort boat and left with a second boat to seek shelter. After surviving 20 miles of the swim, Kathryn Simecek gave up also. Her sister stretched her lead to over 1 mile ahead of Erikson but started to falter. The muscular, well-padded chemist did not seem to notice the wind and waves while steadily maintaining 52 strokes per minute. Korbai also swam well, although lagging ¾ mile behind Ted.

The crew members had a difficult assignment in directing the swimmers since the darkness and waves obscured them. Only at dawn were they to realize that the wind was forcing them far off course to the south.

At 9 p.m. Cynthia, claiming that the waves were too much, joined her sister in the boat. Ted Erikson took over first place and was pursued by Korbai for the next 4 hours. Just after midnight Korbai, too, surrendered to defeat.

Erikson alone battled through the 15- to 20-mile-per-hour winds and towering waves, while on shore reporters and television camera crews booked airplanes and charter boats for dawn. At 7 a.m. when Ted's crew could finally see where they were, they found a terrifying sight—sand dunes! They were about 6 miles from the Indiana State Dune Park, many miles south of their intended destination. In spite of horrendous swimming conditions, Erikson had covered 30 miles but instead of having 6¾ miles to go, he had a long, difficult swim ahead of him up the east coast of Lake Michigan.

Realizing that it would break his spirit to learn this, the crew did not tell Erikson about their costly mistake. Fortunately, the wind died down, and the lake flattened out throughout the morning. By 9 a.m. press boats surrounded the lone swimmer, while movies were shot of him from low flying airplanes. By 1 p.m. Ted was breaststroking less than 1 mile per hour but could see the smokestacks at Michigan City. Nearing exhaustion, he persistently demanded to know how far he still had to go.

Inveterate swimmer Ted Erikson reaches for a new bathing cap being handed him by his wife, Loretta. At this point, two miles from his goal at Michigan City, Indiana, he had been in the water 34 hours, and had another agonizing 2½ hours ahead of him.

By late afternoon it began raining again, and the waves grew to 1½ feet high. With 5 miles for Ted to go, spectator boats homed in on him while teenagers dove in to swim alongside their hero. The amiable but weary Erikson smiled at the cheering crowd, but his crew was certain he would give up soon. His skin looked bluish as he inched along, fighting desperately to finish before nightfall.

By 7 p.m., however, Ted found himself in total darkness and could not see how far away the shoreline was. Neighboring boats focused spotlights on him, stirring him to pick up his stroke slightly although he was still unable to see any landmarks. By 8:30 p.m. the great swimmer, battling 2-foot waves, reached the pier and wearily waved from the water to a monstrous crowd of 30,000 spectators.

When he groaned, "Is this it?" the officials told him that he still had to swim the remaining half mile to the beach. Lungs burning and arms aching, Ted swore in disbelief before allowing the spectators to pull him onto the pier.

The crowd lining the beaches and pier at Michigan City roared when at 8:37 p.m. Ted Erikson came out of the water, the first person ever to swim across Lake Michigan. In spite of merciless waves, rain, wind, and poor navigation, Ted had completed one of the most punishing swims in history in 36 hours 37 minutes. Instead of the original $36\frac{3}{4}$ miles, he had conquered an astounding 44 miles.

Erikson made his way through the ecstatic crowd and walked the $\frac{1}{3}$ mile to the base of the pier. Ambulance attendants wrapped him in blankets and after talking to the press, he was whisked away to a nearby hospital with his loyal fans in close pursuit. When he was weighed in, he discovered that he had lost 17 of his 200 pounds during the ordeal. In the middle of the night Ted suffered through painful spasms requiring muscle relaxants, but by the next day he was well enough to greet his fans.

Although this was Ted's first major competitive event in distance swimming, he walked away with $3,675, a gold-plated trophy, and a $500 gift to start a swimming pool at the Illinois Institute of Technology where he was a part-time swimming coach. Erikson had become famous overnight, and the next few months were to be filled with award ceremonies and speaking engagements. He had doubled the distance of the Catalina or English Channel Swims and launched what was to become an annual event.

1962 Lake Michigan Race

Since Ted Erikson had conquered Lake Michigan in 1961 under the most demanding conditions, the natural follow-up was a race the following year to set a new time and distance record. The same promoter, Jim Moran, offered $4,000 to the first swimmer to reach Waukegan, Illinois, a point $36\frac{3}{4}$ miles north of Chicago. Unlike the previous year, however, this course would follow the shoreline rather than cross the lake, and the race would have two parts. An additional $10,000 was offered to the first athlete to reach Kenosha, Wisconsin, $14\frac{1}{4}$ miles farther north than Waukegan and a total distance of 50 miles from Chicago. If one swimmer was the first to arrive at both points, he would collect still another $10,000.

A total of 20 starters anxiously lined up along the lake the morning of the race. For a change the water appeared placid and warm, registering a tepid 72°F. (22°C.). As the gun was fired, the glassy surface exploded into a frenzy of sprinting swimmers. The names and faces were familiar and included relentless Ted Erikson returning for another record. He was clearly discernible among the bodies due to his smooth, classic-looking stroke and steady 2-mile-per-hour pace. Ahead of him and appearing erratic and uneasy was world renowned Greta Andersen from Denmark (see page 97). From the start the amateurish-looking Chicago lifeguard, Dennis Matuch, took the lead, setting an incredible pace. The hefty swimmer wore no goggles or nose guard and appeared to be on the verge of drowning throughout the race.

For 3 or 4 hours these three great competitors held onto their positions, but Ted fell 2 miles behind Greta. At the end of 25 miles Dennis was still maintaining an exhausting pace but was only a half mile ahead of the Danish superwoman.

As darkness fell over the swimmers, their spirits fell, too, forcing many to drop out in defeat. Greta sprinted frequently in a valiant attempt to catch up to Dennis, but each time she did, the tireless lifeguard pulled away. Suddenly her crafty crew turned off their lights so their opponent could not see her advancing on him. When she finally caught up, Dennis swore at his crew for not warning him and lunged into a powerful, sustained sprint.

In the next half hour he surged a third of a mile ahead of the great Dane and ordered his boat to fall back. As soon as she reached his boat, it dramatically pulled ahead of her to Dennis, thus leaving her demoralized and exhausted. Dennis' entourage used this psychological advantage twice in order to break her spirit.

Apparently, the scheme helped, because 21 hours after leaving Chicago, Dennis Matuch walked ashore at Waukegan to collect $4,000. He had unfalteringly raced through $36\frac{3}{4}$ miles in a world record time that has yet to be

W
I
S
C.

Kenosha

50 Miles

LAKE MICHIGAN

Waukegan

1962 - 36¾ Miles

1963 - 60 Miles

Benton Harbor

MICHIGAN

1961 - 36¾ Miles

Erikson's Course 43-44 Miles
1961

Michigan City

Chicago

ILLINOIS

INDIANA

Gary

Lake Michigan Race routes.

beaten. Since there was no second place reward, Greta Andersen, who was a mere 5 minutes and 300 yards behind the winner, was forced to remain in the water and head for Kenosha.

She slacked off on her frenzied pace considerably and arrived in Kenosha 10 hours later. By completing 50 miles in 31 hours, she set a new world record for open-water swimming. Ted Erikson's classic form brought him into Kenosha 5 hours later, making him co-holder of the distance record.

1963 Lake Michigan Race

The following year, 1963, promoter Moran realized that more prize money was the key to attracting the big-name swimmers. Therefore, he offered the third largest reward in the history of the sport, $15,000, to the first person to cross Lake Michigan from Chicago to Benton Harbor in St. Joseph, Michigan. This would be a much longer distance than Ted Erikson's original crossing since it would total 60 miles.

At a pre-race meeting two days prior to the event, it was evident that many expert swimmers would be competing this time. Garrulous Abo-Heif, in spite of just winning the 15-mile Canadian National Exhibition race the previous day, was present. In that race he had trailed by 13 miles in 55°F. (12.8°C.) water and yet, miraculously had gone on to win. Newlywed

Jumping the gun at the start of the 1963 Lake Michigan swim is Argentinean Syder Guiscardo. Although only 8 a.m., over 400 spectators had turned out.

Cynthia Simecek was also at the meeting discussing the course and the boat assignments. Jim Woods, a 44-year-old businessman and holder of the best record for crossing Lake Ontario, arrived from Florida for the briefing.

Ted Erikson, preparing for his third crossing, asked the doctors at the meeting if he could take cortisone during the race because of a serious leg injury he had suffered 5 weeks prior to the event. Possibly reflecting on Ted's great contributions to the sport, the committee consented. The following morning two Mexicans, Hernandez and Gonzalez, as well as an Argentinean, Syder Guiscardo, were to arrive. Everyone

appeared exceptionally nervous except Abo-Heif who laughed and joked as usual.

At 6:30 a.m. on Tuesday, August 20, the starters began to arrive. The weather cooperated with a clear sky and 76°F. (24.4°C.) air temperature. The lake registered 66°F. (19°C.) and appeared flat. Greta Andersen seemed anxious, Ted Erikson appeared to be deep in thought, and Abo-Heif seemed to be his jovial self, coating his body with thick yellow lanolin and jokingly trying to embrace others with his greasy arms.

About 400 early morning spectators lined the harbor awaiting the 8 a.m. start. When the

Here's Guiscardo again, this time in the water and closing in on white-capped Greta Andersen. By late day Andersen was well ahead and Guiscardo pulled out of the race.

gun fired, adrenaline flowed, the water was white with churning, and the race began. Dennis Matuch flailed away at 90 strokes per minute. Twenty yards behind were Andersen, Abo-Heif, and Guiscardo. Cynthia appeared uneasy, stroking faster than normal, but was already a full 50 yards behind the leader. Ted Erikson, realizing he had to keep up with the leaders, stroked slowly but powerfully. Seven others lagged behind him.

As they left the harbor, Greta, Abo-Heif, and Guiscardo were almost neck and neck while Ted fell farther behind. A frenzied battle developed. As Dennis sprinted ahead of the

others each time one would catch up with him. Ted slowly began to gain on erratic Cynthia and by 8:45 a.m. was only 20 yards behind her.

By 9 a.m. the race had changed significantly, with the pack propelling along as a group past Dennis. Erikson at the same time inched by Cynthia and the leaders left the other competitors far behind. By 9:30 a.m. Ted was gradually closing in on the faltering Dennis who was now fourth, a full two blocks behind the leaders.

Abo-Heif and his two competitors were stroking erratically and kicking abnormally hard due to their prolonged sprinting. Every 10 minutes one would pressure the other by sprinting ahead of the pack. Suddenly, $2\frac{1}{2}$ hours into the race Abo-Heif surged ahead, with Greta Andersen close behind, but Guiscardo fell slightly back. Their tactics worked well, and at the end of a half hour the Argentinean lagged a quarter of a mile behind.

Meanwhile Dennis Matuch and Ted Erikson gained on the unsteady Guiscardo. Stopping to take his first feeding, Abo-Heif swam in front of Greta, thus disrupting her pace. As soon as he ate, he immediately caught up with her, and she then took her feeding. Even though they each had 53 miles ahead of them, neither would allow the other to take over first place.

During this race a plane flew over every 4 hours to be sure they were on course. At regular intervals crew members told each swimmer their stroke rate and the weather conditions ahead. At 1 p.m. the placid lake registered 69°F. (20.6°C.). Ted and Dennis stopped for their first feeding, but when they re-entered the race, a change took place with Ted suddenly increasing his pace, leaving Dennis behind. During the next hour Erikson slowly but persistently gained on Guiscardo and finally caught up. Greta and Abo-Heif, a mile and a half in front of Ted, maintained a slightly faster pace.

At 4:05 p.m. Guiscardo quit, and Dennis lagged far back. Erikson had a firm grip on third place but was downing cortisone pills regularly. At 7:45 p.m. Dennis, a full mile behind Ted, unexpectedly left the race. As darkness fell, visibility declined forcing Erikson to swim dangerously close to his escort boat.

Suddenly, after $13\frac{1}{2}$ hours of intensive swimming, Greta Andersen pulled herself out of the water and the race. About 2 hours earlier the Egyptian had sprinted into a 15-yard lead, and Greta had been unable to equal his effort. He mercilessly pulled away from her during the next $1\frac{1}{2}$ hours, forcing Greta to realize that she did not have a chance of winning and that a second place prize of $2,000 was not worth the struggle.

By this time only the invincible Abo-Heif and a determined Ted Erikson remained in the water. The usual uncertainties and doubts that infiltrate swimmers at night swept over the two competitors. Abo-Heif seemed to be having trouble and asked for a swimming cap, but Erikson's boat refused to help. At 11 p.m. Ted's crew shrewdly turned off its boat lights to confuse the Egyptian.

Over the next 3 hours Erikson swam steadily and powerfully and by 2 a.m. was able to see the lights on Abo-Heif's boat. At 4 a.m. with the leader only two blocks in front, several race officials pulled alongside Ted and his crew and demanded that they turn their lights back on.

At dawn Ted's crew discerned Abo-Heif's boat about a mile ahead, but fog and haze immediately shrouded it from view. At one time Ted drew to within $\frac{3}{4}$ of a mile of his opponent but did not know it. By this point the Egyptian was stopping for feedings only every 2 to 3 hours since he knew Ted was close behind. Erikson stopped infrequently for his feeding of nutriment laced with pablum, egg yolks, and cortisone pills. His leg was a severe handicap for when he swam too hard, he suffered cramps.

At 1:30 p.m. an excursion boat, overflowing with jubilant, cheering Egyptians, pulled alongside Abo-Heif to offer encouragement. The leader, racing against daylight as well as a strong opponent, needed this mental lift. By 3 p.m. the Egyptian was within 6 miles of the finish and Ted, a full 10 miles away, realized Abo-Heif would win.

At 6:30 p.m. jovial Abo-Heif tore off his goggles, waved to the spectators, and started swimming back towards Chicago. The amiable clown back-stroked in order to get a better view of the crowd watching his antics.

At 6:43 p.m. the smiling champion stumbled and sprinted from the water into the crowd of admirers. Waving away the stretcher, he walked along the beach for 20 minutes shaking hands and talking to reporters. Abo-Heif had become the world champion.

Meanwhile Ted Erikson's crew reluctantly

The victory parade out of the water—jubilant Abdel-Latif Abo-Heif of Egypt, flanked by his wife and race promoter Jim Moran. Mrs. Abo-Heif is waving a United Arab Republic flag.

told him that he had lost, but the relentless swimmer maintained his pace anyway. Two hours and 53 minutes later, Ted became a co-holder of the distance record Abo-Heif had set.

While the Egyptian was taken to a Chicago hotel for a brief rest, Ted was taken to a local hospital. Suffering from severe muscle spasms, Erikson was given injections and sleeping pills to ease his pain. Abo-Heif's wife later admitted that the invincible winner had also endured great pain that night.

A total of $40,000 was awarded by Moran for the 1963 swim, but it was to be the last Lake Michigan crossing, due to increased expenses and growing public indifference.

21. Lake St. John Swim and 24-Hour La Tuque Swim

In 1955, a local Canadian named Jacques Amyot became famous overnight among his countrymen by completing an unprecedented swim across Lake St. John. The 28-mile-long, 19-mile-wide lake in the middle of Quebec Province had never previously been conquered. A hero in his home town of Roberval, Jacques was interviewed frequently on television. During the following two years another Canadian, Paul Des Ruisseaux, set new records for the crossing, and in 1957 his record swim attracted more than 10,000 spectators.

The local merchants, of course, profited greatly from the influx of fans and therefore decided to formalize the event into a race the following year. In addition to cash prizes, they offered the athletes paid expenses for one week prior to the race. The event was publicized widely and attracted over 25,000 enthusiastic spectators. That first year the race was won by Greta Andersen and was a financial success.

The following year grandstands were erected on the shoreline overlooking swimming lanes so that the spectators could watch the final mile of the event. To add even more drama to the race, in 1965, officials turned the last mile into a sprint by awarding prizes for the fastest mile. That year over 50,000 sports fans witnessed the race.

Over the years, marathon swimming grew increasingly popular in Canada, and in 1969

Prime Minister Pierre Trudeau was the official starter of the Lake St. John Swim. The following year five swimmers sprinted through the final mile together with the crowd going berserk.

Promoters throughout Canada and the world began to realize in the early 1960's that great financial profits could be reaped from marathon swimming. A group of businessmen in the tiny town of La Tuque, Quebec, decided that if their neighbor, Roberval, could do it, so could they. Unfortunately, they did not have a huge lake in which to stage a race, but they did have a small, block-long, spring-fed lake in their park.

The ingenious men of La Tuque struck on the idea of setting up buoys and having swimmers race each other around the lake for 24 hours. To make it even more exciting, the competitors would form two-man teams. Such a set-up would allow spectators for the first time in the history of the sport to witness an entire marathon swim.

The first race was to be held July 24–25, 1965, and would run from 3 p.m. Saturday to 3 p.m. Sunday. The rules were that a swimmer had to complete at least one lap, a little over $\frac{1}{3}$ mile, before his teammate could relieve him. He could also swim as many laps as he wanted before resting. The lake was a comfortable 72°F. (22°C.), but later that night it seemed to

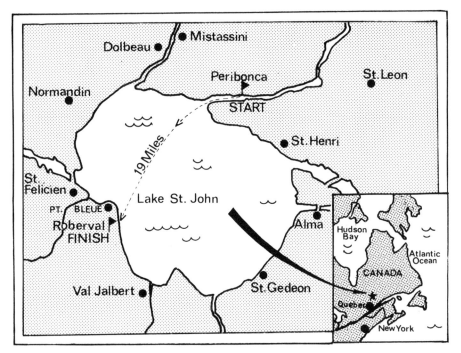

Route of the Lake St. John Swim.

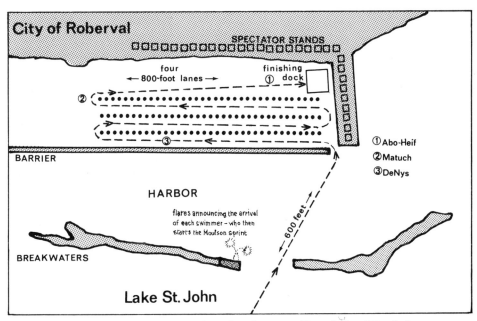

What the swimmer competing in the grueling Lake St. John race finds awaiting him at the finish . . . a one-mile sprint. Here you can see the frenzied 1970 sprint through the lanes which took place before a wildly cheering crowd of 50,000.

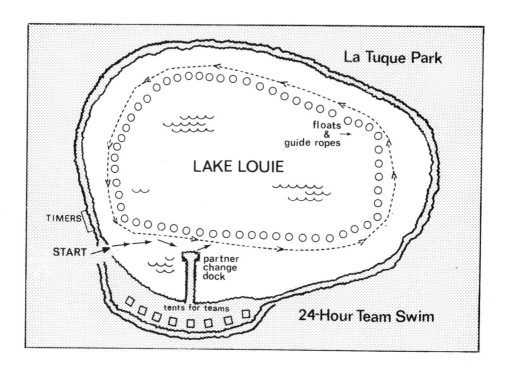

the exhausted competitors to be as frigid as an ocean swim.

Before the start of the race thousands of people flocked to tiny Lake Louie, many seeking autographs from their idols. The Egyptian team of Abo-Heif and Shazly were there as were the favorites, Ted Erikson and Dennis Matuch. Erikson had crossed Lake Michigan three times already, and Matuch had won the 36-mile Lake Michigan race in 1962. Herman Willemse and his teammate, John LaCoursiere, were present also but they had never attempted such great distances.

From the start of the race the differences in strategies were readily apparent. LaCoursiere and Willemse maintained a fast pace by swimming only one lap at a time. The Egyptian team fell in behind these two, followed by Erikson and Matuch who were cautiously pacing themselves.

When the gun signaled the end of the grueling ordeal the following afternoon, LaCoursiere and

Willemse collected the $3,500 first prize after completing 55 miles. The Egyptians were a full 3 miles behind them, and surprisingly the favored team of Erikson and Matuch had covered only 45 miles.

The unique 24-hour marathon was a great financial success for the local merchants and sponsors. It has been held every year since 1965 and has provided many exciting moments for the thousands of spectators who witness it.

The 1974 race typified the drama that commonly unfurls. As the sports fans downed bottle after bottle of beer while enthusiastically cheering through a chain-link fence, 15 or so teams battled it out in Lake Louie for first place. On Sunday morning one weary swimmer, who was sobbing and complaining of stomach cramps, was picked up and thrown into the race. He merely touched his teammate's hand and began swimming mechanically.

Another athlete suffering greatly was 21-year-old John Kinsella. The 6-foot-4-inch, 204-

pound NCAA champion was in his first professional race and could not handle the intense cold. By midnight he and his female partner, Sandy Bucha of Indiana, were leading by three laps, but he was spending more and more time in his tent under a pile of blankets. By this time Kinsella, who had won both a silver and a gold medal in the 1968 and 1972 Olympics respectively, now seriously wondered what he was doing in La Tuque. He simply could not stop shivering even with a tent over his head and a doctor by his side.

Young and pretty Sandy Bucha had failed to qualify for the Olympics, but in 1973 had broken the previous record for the 10-mile Lake Michigan Swim. Unfortunately, in that race Johans Schans, the former record holder, also broke his record and captured first place.

Sandy swam extremely well in the La Tuque marathon and admitted that those laps were much less tiring than the sprints she usually did. While she and John Kinsella gulped fructose tablets throughout the race, other swimmers swallowed corn syrup, hot chocolate, tea, glucose, cookies, and jelly. By 1 a.m. Kinsella was shivering violently in his tent even though he had found a heater. Sandy was feeling better than ever so she swam longer, slower laps.

By 3 a.m. the swimmers could stroke gracefully through the water but on land could not focus their bloodshot eyes or even walk. Unlike the others, at dawn Sandy's eyes sparkled brightly as she posed for cameramen. Kinsella was unable even to smile and was only swimming two laps for every three that Sandy did. In spite of his problems the team lengthened their lead over the second-place competitors.

By the 16th hour of the non-stop swim, Kinsella's left thigh throbbed from a pulled tendon. The doctor admonished him for swimming too fast since lactic acid was building up in his muscles. By then Sandy looked as if she had aged overnight and had large, dark circles beneath her eyes. Even Dennis Matuch, who had competed in all ten La Tuque races, now looked as if near death.

At 8 a.m. Diana Nyad (see page 113), one of the world's top female swimmers, was rushed to a hospital. As she lay unconscious, glucose was dripped intravenously into one arm, and vitamins were injected into the other. Her determined partner, Marcello Guiscardo, announced that he would finish the race alone.

Meanwhile Sandy Bucha was swimming four lap stints since John was unable even to leave his tent. At noon the townspeople converged on the tiny lake, and a carnival-like atmosphere prevailed. Beer flowed freely while music blared from loudspeakers and transistors. At 1:14 p.m. the Kinsella team broke the previous distance record by completing lap 181. The water was a balmy 75°F. (24°C.), but the thoroughly chilled Kinsella got out and headed for the tent.

By this time Diana Nyad was back from the hospital, pleading with her partner to let her back in the race. Guiscardo, however, swimming with the use of only one arm and apparently trying to prove himself, refused to get out of the water.

At 3 p.m. when a cannon was fired to signal the end of the race, Sandy Bucha was completing her 100th lap. The second-place swimmer, Johans Schans, had finished 90 while John Kinsella, having maintained a fantastic $3\frac{1}{4}$-mile-per-hour pace, had completed 94 laps. Bucha and Kinsella seemed to blossom in the sunshine and forget all the pain as they were awarded the $3,500 first prize.

Sometimes swimmers are totally incapacitated in marathons such as this. In the 1966 30-hour race in Montreal, Abo-Heif gallantly took over for his partner, Travaglio, when the latter became too cold to continue. The astounding Egyptian swam 29 of the 30 hours unassisted and dramatically captured first place.

Tirelessly churning through the waters of the English Channel, Florence Chadwick is on her way to breaking the record Gertrude Ederle held for 24 years by 1 hour 11 minutes. The year is 1950.

22. Queen of the World's Waterways: Florence Chadwick

The success of the great Florence Chadwick was founded on early failure. At the tender age of 6 she entered her first race and placed last out of seven starters. It was only a 50-yard sprint, but she cried and insisted on racing again to prove she could do better. With her father acting as coach, she worked out in the ocean off San Diego and when landbound, she sawed trees to build up her arms.

When Chadwick was barely 10 years old, she swam the San Diego Bay Channel, and at 11 won her first race. Her mother escorted her to her daily workouts in a bay near her home and watched her swim her heart out for the next few years. At 14, Florence placed second in the Nationals and won many sectional titles.

Two years later, as a husky high school teenager, she threw a crowd of spectators at Oceanside, California, into panic with her unconventional racing tactics. As her fellow swimmers plunged into the surf for a 3-mile event, Chadwick veered to the right and was suddenly caught in a turbulent riptide which dragged her away from shore. These powerful currents take the lives of hundreds of bathers each year.

The spectators screamed, watching her being pulled farther out with each stroke. A patrol boat sped to her rescue, but suddenly she worked free from the current and headed for the first buoy in the race. She swam smoothly and easily won the race by 300 yards. When a spectator asked if she had been afraid, astonished she replied, "Oh, no! I always ride a riptide if I can find one."

Chadwick and her father had spotted the riptide prior to the race and merely worked it into her racing strategy. She knew that it would carry her several hundred yards out and then dissipate. Those that drown each year do so only because they fight the current rather than ride with it.

Chadwick never placed better than second in national events and, in 1936, she placed a discouraging fourth in the Olympic trials, barely missing the team. Believing that she was a failure, Florence went on to college and eventually marriage. She then turned professional and in 1945 swam in MGM's Esther Williams' movie, "Bathing Beauty."

Thinking that her swimming career was finally behind her, she began studying law and coaching at the La Jolla Beach and Tennis Club. One day, however, while glancing at an old scrapbook, Chadwick noticed a motto she had pasted there as a young girl: "Winners never quit; quitters never win." Suddenly realizing that she had given up after 20 years of training, she decided to return to swimming.

This time, however, she would only attempt long distance ocean conquests since this was her strongest area.

Chadwick's first goal was to cross the English Channel as her idol, Gertrude Ederle, had once done. (See page 57.) To earn money for this excursion, Florence worked in Saudi Arabia, in addition to swimming 6 hours each day in the Persian Gulf. In 1950, she moved to France and practiced in the waters off Wissant.

Chadwick went almost unnoticed as she struck out for Dover on August 8 of that year in a valiant attempt to break Ederle's 24-year-old record. The London *Daily Mail* was sponsoring a contest that day but would not even let her enter since they felt she did not have a chance. All eyes were on 17-year-old Shirley May France who was also attempting the crossing.

Eventually France was pulled from the water in tears. Florence Chadwick battled through the same strong tides that were the undoing of her opponent, and she was carried far off course. Drifting into the British artillery practice area, she inadvertently forced them to stop firing. Finally the determined woman fought through the remaining 3 miles in a strenuous, painful 4 hours. After 13 hours 20 minutes, Chadwick walked ashore at Dover and became the new holder of the women's record for crossing the English Channel. She had beaten Gertrude Ederle's 1926 record by 1 hour 11 minutes. She also became the 32nd person and 13th woman to conquer the famous waterway.

Her renewed interest in swimming seemed well worth the sacrifices when she returned home to find thousands of fans and a ticker-tape parade greeting her in San Diego. She was awarded a bouquet of flowers and a car, which was fortunate because she was broke, having spent all of her savings on the Channel swim.

The following year was a challenging one also as Chadwick attempted to break a 25-year-old record for the 21-mile channel swim from Santa Catalina Island to Los Angeles. No

Florence has a lot to smile about—she has just completed the treacherous Santa Catalina Island swim, the first woman to accomplish the feat and the first athlete to beat the 25-year-old record made by George Young in 1927.

woman had ever accomplished this feat, and Florence was determined to be the first.

In her ill-fated first attempt, she was blinded by fog and unable to see any reassuring landmarks. After 16 hours in the surf and only 1 mile from shore, she quit. Florence was again inspired, however, when she received 3,000 encouraging letters from fans who had watched her on television.

On September 20, 1952, she set out again under better weather conditions. This time 55,000,000 people viewed her progress on television. Although her crew members had to shoot at sharks circling dangerously close by, she continued on. Florence suffered through stomach cramps, but her brother, Richard, kept her spirits high. At feeding time he

donned a chef's hat, clanged a dinner bell, and fed her lumps of sugar one by one.

After 13 hours 14 minutes Chadwick stumbled ashore at Point Vincente cutting her feet and legs on the rocks. Although she had reduced George Young's record by 2 hours, all she collected for her gallant efforts was a few thousand dollars from television rights, endorsements, and contributions. She later said that her greatest reward was in showing millions of youngsters the road to good health, sportsmanship, and safety in the water.

Chadwick's swimming skills saved her in the ocean many times. One day during a practice swim off Santa Monica a fog bank suddenly engulfed her. She swam for 2 hours not knowing which direction to turn to reach shore. She strained to pick out sounds coming from land but heard nothing. Realizing that panic takes more lives than exhaustion, she remained calm remembering that the ocean was her friend. She confidently took off in one direction and fortunately found her way back to shore.

In 1953, Florence Chadwick reached the peak of her swimming career by conquering four channels in 5 weeks and setting new records in all of them. Her first challenge was the crossing of the English Channel from Dover to Cape Gris-Nez. She set out from England just before midnight on September 3 in spite of the predictions of the experts that it was a bad time to attempt a crossing. She had postponed the swim countless times and her English residence permit had already expired. She had promised in the press, "I'm going to give you menfolk something to shoot at," and could not back out now.

Maintaining a straight course in spite of the strong tidal currents, Chadwick reached Wissant, France, in a record 14 hours 42 minutes. After a 4-minute break to eat an orange, she astounded everyone by getting back in the chilly water and heading for England. Florence was attempting to complete the first double crossing of the English Channel in history. On her return trip, however, she was stung painfully by a mass of jellyfish and was forced to quit after only $2\frac{1}{4}$ miles.

On September 20, 1953, Chadwick swam the Strait of Gibraltar in a mere 5 hours 6 minutes. On October 7 she completed a round-trip swim across the Bosporus (in Turkey between Europe and Asia) in a record 1 hour 14 minutes.

Two days later Florence retraced the route across the Turkish Dardanelles (the Hellespont) which Leander of Greek mythology had taken each night to visit his love, Hero. Chadwick completed her grand slam conquest of four channels in 5 weeks by arriving in Canakkale, Turkey, in a record time of 1 hour 58 minutes.

Following this final swim, Florence Chad-wick, then 33 years old, announced her retirement from marathon swimming by saying, "This is a sport for younger people. I think I'll take up golf." Her retirement was short-lived, however, for the following year, 1954, she attempted her most challenging swim ever. At 4:45 a.m. on an August morning, the irrepressible swimmer entered the notorious, icy Strait of Juan de Fuca with the intention of becoming the first person ever to swim the $18\frac{1}{2}$ miles between Victoria, British Columbia, and Port Angeles, Washington.

After going less than a quarter of the way across and having suffered in the 48°F. (9°C.) water for a bitter 5 hours 11 minutes, Chadwick was pulled from the sea. Although she was blue from the cold, she claimed that it was the powerful currents which stopped her.

Only three other attempts had previously

Another record for Chadwick. Here Florence reaches for a nourishing beverage during a pause in her 1953 English Channel crossing which she made in 14 hours 42 minutes. Although she almost immediately turned around and started a return trip after touching down in France, she was forced to quit after being stung by jellyfish.

After the English Channel, the Strait of Gibraltar was a breeze for the indomitable Florence Chadwick. On September 20, 1953, she made the crossing from Spain to Africa in the record time of 5 hours 6 minutes.

been made on the Strait and all had been failures. Chadwick, the only female among them, stayed in the water longer and swam farther than the others. A prize of $7,500 had been offered by local sponsors for any attempt on the waterway with an extra $2,500 thrown in for a successful crossing. The sponsors, however, were so impressed with Florence's determination that they awarded her the entire $10,000.

In 1955, Chadwick swam the English Channel from England to France for the third time setting a new record in 13 hours 33 minutes.

Throughout the late 1950's, Florence Chadwick was probably the highest paid woman athlete in the country due to the five figure income she earned from radio and television programs, endorsements, as well as exhibition swims. Today she is the only female stockbroker in San Diego and spends her weekends training young Sandra Keshka, a member of the new generation of Channel swimmers (see page 92).

The 5-foot-6-inch 140-pound Florence Chadwick conquered 16 channels and set many new records in her short career. In addition, she destroyed the misconception that only men and very well-padded women can withstand the cold endured in marathon swimming.

In 1954, Mac Davis awarded Florence the appropriate title, "Queen of the World's Waterways."

23. Danish Superwoman: Greta Andersen

The handsome, broad-shouldered Dane, Greta Andersen, appears to have been built for marathon swimming. At 5 feet 10 inches and varying from 145 to 168 pounds this superwoman has beaten every man she has ever competed against in professional swimming at least once. She may possibly hold more records than any swimmer of either sex in the world.

When born in Copenhagen, Denmark, in 1930, she weighed an awesome 12 pounds. Greta inherited her athletic prowess from her father who was the gymnastic champion of Denmark. She also had an older brother who held the Danish bicycle championship for 5 years.

Greta began her lengthy swimming career at the age of 15 when she enrolled in a swimming school. Within six months she became the second fastest swimmer in Denmark, and over the next two years Greta broke every Danish swimming record and even some international ones in the girls' divisions. She had no trouble qualifying for the 1948 Olympics in London and proceeded to capture a gold medal in the 100-meter free-style. She also helped the Danish relay team capture second place in the 400-meter event.

After the Olympics Greta finished high school and continued amateur swimming. By the end of her amateur career, she had collected 35 Copenhagen, 24 Danish, and four European championships in addition to setting two world records, one (a 100-yard event) which lasted for 7 years.

When Greta was 20 years old, however, she needed money and went to the United States to perform exhibition swimming. In 1953, she moved to Glendale, California, to become a swimming instructor.

One day while working out in Long Beach, California, Greta met a few members of a nearby swim club who introduced her to the world of marathon swimming. Prior to that she had been unaware that such competition existed. They talked for hours of the conquest of the nearby Catalina Channel and mentioned a marathon to be held in 3 months in California's Salton Sea. Greta became intrigued and decided to race in the 10.5-mile event.

The 30-mile-long Salton Sea lies in a burning hot, desolate part of southern California, entirely surrounded by desert. On the day of the race (April 29, 1956) the water temperature was a debilitating 78°F. (25.5°C.). Greta had averaged 6 to 8 miles per day in preparing for her first marathon, and although she was beaten by several men in the race, she set a women's record for the course in 4 hours 25 minutes. The ebullient Scandinavian loved the race and decided that it was much more fulfilling than the shorter ones.

Andersen's next competition was the much publicized Atlantic City marathon. In that race she established herself in marathon swimming circles by finishing first among the women and placing fourth only 26 minutes behind the winner.

In 1957, Greta breezed through the 15-mile Huntington Beach to Long Beach, California, marathon in 6 hours 14 minutes, again becoming the first woman to finish. The next swim was a 26-mile event which started from a point on the west coast of the Gulf of California and ended around the peninsula in the harbor at Guaymas, Mexico. Andersen, completing the 26 miles in 12 hours, placed second behind the Canadian, Tom Park.

On July 25 of that year Greta again came in behind Park by taking third place in the Atlantic City Swim. The following month she set a new record for the 15-mile Owen Sound Marathon in Canada in a time of 6 hours 15 minutes. The previous record, 7 hours 33 minutes, had been set by a man 24 years earlier.

In that same hectic month, the superwoman competed against 24 athletes in the English Channel race and collected the first prize of $3,000 in Dover after swimming 13 hours 53 minutes. Only one other swimmer was able to battle the 3½-foot waves to finish the brutal race, and he arrived more than 2 hours later. With this victory Greta became known worldwide.

After the race she returned to the United States, got married, and continued to swim competitively. Her first race in 1958 was the Guaymas, Mexico, event. Greta trained religiously, knowing that she would need top speed to beat the ever-present Tom Park, who was to become one of the best swimmers of that year.

The Guaymas race became a personal battle between Park and Andersen, with the two of them swimming neck and neck most of the way. After a torturous 6 hours, Greta pulled in front, however, and never relinquished her lead. As she entered the harbor at Guaymas, no other swimmers were in sight. Greta won easily with only 18 of the 27 starters even finishing the event.

In the July 14 Atlantic City contest Tom Park and Cliff Lumsden captured first and second places, leaving third for Greta. The following month Greta collected her third win

Her body still coated with grease, Greta Andersen steadies herself after crawling out of the water at Dover—the winner of a Channel race in a field of 24.

against men in a professional race. This occurred on August 2 in the 19-mile Lake St. John Marathon which she won in 8 hours 17 minutes. At that time no other women were even swimming in that particular event. Greta Andersen completed the 1958 professional circuit by winning the English Channel race in 10 hours 59 minutes and becoming the only swimmer ever to win it twice.

When she arrived home from her lengthy tour, Greta began planning a double crossing of the San Pedro Channel (Catalina Swim) for publicity. This feat had never been accomplished previously and was an awesome undertaking.

On October 5, 1958, Andersen dove from Santa Catalina Island into Emerald Bay and set out on a straight 19-mile course for Point Vincente. The water was flat and an appeasing 72°F. (22°C.), but after 3 hours a dense fog engulfed Greta. Unimpeded by this, the Dane reached her destination in a world record time of 10 hours 49 minutes.

Faced with the return trip, Greta became nervous and reluctant. Her trainer-husband and her crew were worried also, for they spent almost 20 minutes trying to talk her out of it. Finally, the courageous woman got up and re-entered the water in spite of her sore muscles and faltering attitude. She endured for many hours, but the lengthy swim was taking its toll on her nerves. Although exhausted and racked with pain, Greta continued on. Her crew worried about her vacant eyes and blank expression and knew she could not break the world record for the mainland to Catalina direction. After a painful 15 hours 38 minutes, Greta did manage to complete the crossing but took much longer than Tom Park's 1956 one-way swim. His record time was 9 hours 10 minutes.

Andersen still managed to establish two new records: one for the fastest time from the island to the mainland and the other for the first successful double crossing of the San Pedro Channel. The latter record, 38 miles in 26 hours 53 minutes, still stands today.

In 1959, Greta returned to being a winner of just the women's divisions of the great races. The outcome of the July 17 Atlantic City race was becoming routine. Although she kept pace with the leaders until the last 2 miles, they mercilessly pulled away leaving her to claim third place. Cliff Lumsden finished in 10 hours 54 minutes 5 seconds; Tom Park came in second with a time of 11:07:15; and Greta was close behind with a time of 11:07:25. The story was the same at the Capri-Naples event and the English Channel race—third place for Greta.

In 1960, Greta did not score any record times. That year at the age of 30 she went to Hawaii with her husband to attempt for the

second time a crossing of the unconquered channel between the islands of Molokai and Oahu. The previous year Greta had attempted this swim but was defeated by the strong currents. This year she came back to Hawaii with television support and an assortment of contracts. If this solo swim had been successful, the publicity would have been converted into five times as much money as she could win in a professional race.

Greta made a daring attempt on the Molokai Channel while her navigator maneuvered her through the currents. During the exhausting 18 hours of swimming, the great athlete was relentlessly pushed off course by the currents. She eventually was forced to abandon the expedition short of her goal. Only one year later a local swimmer, Keo Nakama, used excellent navigation, as well as his own outstanding skill, to conquer the channel during neap tide.

In 1961, Greta began a new policy of dropping out of races when she could not collect any prize money. The Canadian National Exhibition race was the only one that year which she completed, and she captured third prize. In 1962, Greta lost third place to LaCoursiere in the Lake St. John Marathon. She finished a mere 6 minutes behind him.

In spite of this disappointment, the tireless Dane went directly to a little known race in 1962 in Chicago—the Lake Michigan Race. In that 36/50-mile event, she won the title of World's Long Distance Open Water Swimming Champion. In that dramatic competition (described in Chapter 20) Greta lagged only a few minutes behind the winner of the 36-mile race, Dennis Matuch. She eventually lost the first stage by only several hundred yards but went on to win $10,000 for completing the 50-mile event.

In 1963, Greta completed her final season of professional swimming at the age of 33. She finished fifth in the Atlantic City race, beating the young and talented Marty Sinn (see page 107) by only 17 minutes. At the C.N.E. races

The Danish superwoman glides through the Pacific en route back to Catalina Island after setting a new record for the Catalina-to-mainland swim. Although physically and mentally exhausted, she managed to complete the return trip.

later that year Marty swam past Greta after only 3 miles, causing the Scandinavian to give up in disgust.

On August 21, 1963, Greta entered the ill-fated 60-mile Lake Michigan marathon (described on page 83). After she battled it out for 12 hours with the great Egyptian swimmer, Abo-Heif, he finally picked up his pace, leaving her behind. Realizing that 45 miles of cold water stretched between her and the finish, Greta called her escort boat over and was pulled out of the race, after 13½ hours in the water.

In 1964, Greta entered but did not complete the Lake Ontario marathon, the final profes-

sional race of her career. That same year and the following one she was enticed back to the English Channel for three more attempts at a double crossing. Each time she completed the first crossing, but never was successful in the second.

Ted Erikson became the second swimmer in history to complete the double crossing and did it only a few weeks after Greta's final failure in 1965. Greta Andersen literally threw in the towel after that and ended her 20-year professional swimming career. Greta is still involved in swimming, however, for in addition to being the wife of a Los Angeles doctor, she owns a very successful swim school.

24. Lady of the Lake: Marilyn Bell

In addition to Cliff Lumsden and Tom Park, Toronto's Lakeshore Swim Club spawned another great athlete, the 5-foot-2-inch 119-pound Marilyn Bell. Marilyn, a likeable schoolgirl who sang in the church choir and loved badminton, had joined the successful club at the age of 9. From the beginning she realized that she was not as fast as others her age but enjoyed swimming so much that she spent every winter in the club pool and every summer in Lake Ontario.

Over the years Marilyn grew to idolize Gus Ryder, the club's director, and Cliff Lumsden, the five-time winner of the C.N.E. races. Realizing that she could not win shorter events, she began tagging along with Cliff on his 5- to 15-mile training swims.

In 1954, Marilyn, Gus Ryder, and Tom Park entered the Atlantic City marathon (page 75), a 25-mile swim around Absecon Island in New Jersey. This was the first year of the popular race, and the Toronto teenager was the first female to finish, placing seventh. Fellow Canadians, Park and Lumsden, finished first and second, only 3 minutes apart.

Their next major competition that year was the Canadian National Exhibition race which in 1954 was a team event. Organizers believed that a team effort would generate more excitement than a standard marathon. Each competitor was to swim as many laps as he wanted and then be relieved by a team member. The winning team was to collect $10,000.

The Canadians captured the first prize that year by completing the 30-mile course in 13 hours. Although Marilyn was an alternate to the winning team, she did not swim with them but was busy making history instead.

The Canadian National Exhibition had contracted with the world's greatest female swimmer of the time, Florence Chadwick, to stage a special event at the fair that year. Florence was to be awarded $10,000 for becoming the first person ever to swim across Lake Ontario. When Marilyn heard about the attempt, she pleaded with her coach to allow her to try the crossing for "the honor of Canada."

When Marilyn dove from the Coast Guard station in Youngstown, New York, at 11 p.m. on September 6, 1954, she did not have the assurance of a prize awaiting her at the other side even if successful. The C.N.E. officials had not offered her a reward and in fact she almost went unnoticed in Chadwick's wake.

A third woman also entered the water that night. She was Mrs. Winnie Roach Leuszler, a 28-year-old friend of Marilyn's and the only Canadian woman to conquer the English Channel. A few photographers followed these two women at the start, but the spotlights centered on Chadwick. Winnie started 17 minutes behind Marilyn and soon became lost among the photographers' boats. Unable to locate her escort boat after an hour, she was forced to turn back and start again from the dock. She eventually made it two-thirds of the way across Lake Ontario but finally conceded defeat. Meanwhile, Marilyn stroked through the confusion of boats and headed for the narrow beam of light shining from the National Exhibition, 32 miles across the lake.

The young teenager feared swimming in darkness but continued on through the eerie, unfamiliar waters. Suddenly, something grabbed onto her bathing suit. It was a slimy, determined lamprey eel, hitching a free ride with the solitary swimmer. Marilyn had encountered these pests during practice swims and quickly slipped her thumbnail under the fish's suckers, tossing it away. She remembered when her friend, Cliff Lumsden, had done this with a persistent eel, but it had returned again and again. Finally Cliff had pulled it off, crushed its head between his teeth, and threw the lamprey away once and for all. Marilyn's lamprey never came back.

Soon Marilyn heard her coach's voice and swam toward it. She narrowly missed being struck by the dinghy tied to her escort boat. If she had touched it, she would have been disqualified from the race. A reliable crew consisting of coach Gus Ryder and three others greeted Marilyn in a boat stocked with 8 pounds of corn syrup and a carton of pablum.

Marilyn and Chadwick, unable to see each other, swam through the night while battling choppy, towering waves. During the first hour and a half Marilyn passed her competitor in the dark but neither the swimmers nor their crews realized this until the next morning. When Marilyn and Florence were 3 miles out from Youngstown, they entered open water

Racked with pain and suffering severe depression, 16-year-old Marilyn strokes on just four miles short of her goal. She made it and became the first swimmer in history to cross Lake Ontario.

and hit large, cold, rolling swells. The teenager stopped every hour for a quick feeding but by 4 a.m. had been awake for a total of 18 hours since before the start of the marathon and now suffered from the lack of sleep. She complained first of stomach cramps and then of arm and leg pains. Her coach insisted that she continue, but he started feeding her less often and let her slow her pace slightly. She thought of her parents in the nearby cabin cruiser and of the warmth of the ship's soft berth.

Meanwhile, the veteran swimmer, Florence Chadwick, was vomiting from oil slicks and rolling swells. By 4 a.m. she was hardly swimming at all, and by 5 a.m. Chadwick could barely tread water. Finally 45 minutes later her trainers reluctantly pulled the ailing swimmer on board, and the airways carried the news of her defeat.

By dawn Marilyn had conquered 14 miles in the 7 hours, but her coach was horrified at what the early morning light revealed. Her skin was gray, her lips blue, and her glazed eyes appeared vacant. A crew member insisted that she be pulled from the race. She was unable to move her legs at all and was barely progressing through the chilling water.

Her coach, Gus Ryder, reluctantly told her to get on board the escort boat. Marilyn, realizing that she was defeated after so many hours of swimming, tearfully swam toward him. Suddenly Gus shouted, "Pull away!" The boat lurched from her grasp as Gus yelled to her that her legs were suddenly moving again. Using trickery such as this, the loyal coach kept the young athlete going.

At 7:15 a.m. he passed her a cup of liniment to warm her legs. She smeared the grease on by lifting each leg out of the water and letting her head drop under. The liniment helped, but her stomach cramps persisted. By mid-morning the sun brightened the sky as well as her spirits, and she swam well. Boats brimming with reporters drifted nearby now that Chadwick was out of the contest. They witnessed a historic undertaking by the persistent youngster who continued to battle 10-foot waves and strong currents. Throughout the night and early morning she was mercilessly swept westward off course making the swim a full 10 miles longer than planned.

At 10:30 a.m. Marilyn tried to drink some corn syrup but was shaking so violently that she dropped her cup. She looked up and saw a nearby reporter crying, and suddenly realized that she was doing the same. Her spirits were dropping to the lowest point of the entire swim, so Gus chose this moment to write on the blackboard, "Flo is out." He had saved this news for just such a moment, and it worked well, causing her to sprint a few strokes.

At 3 p.m. Marilyn went into another severe depression and for 20 minutes made no progress at all. Her crew talked to her, but she only responded with tears. Suddenly, Marilyn heard voices and saw new shapes off to each side. She had passed the halfway point and watercraft of every dimension came to accompany her. Ironically those who wanted to assist her actually became a severe hindrance since the oil leaking from their boats was nauseating. Within a half hour she was deathly sick and sleepy, not having slept for 31 hours.

At 4:30 p.m. Marilyn was half asleep and thought she was dreaming when she heard the voice of a friend, Joan Cooke. Her coach, realizing she was failing fast, had sent one of the boats to Toronto to persuade Joan to come to the swimmer's aid. Marilyn, lost in a deep depression and thinking she was alone, awoke suddenly to the sound of a splash nearby. She looked over and found Joan, wearing street clothes, swimming alongside her. While the two friends cried and laughed, the desperate measure helped the youngster regain her rhythm. Joan got out of the water 20 minutes later while Marilyn continued on, refreshed.

At 6 p.m. the lights were visible at the site of the Exhibition. Soon afterward Gus wrote on his blackboard, "2 miles to go," but Marilyn was too tired to be encouraged. As the setting sun reflected off the buildings ahead, Marilyn plodded along on the verge of unconscious-ness. For the final mile of the swim, rockets lit up the skies and thousands of spectators on shore cheered. The weary swimmer had no knowledge of the elapsed time, until she touched the Toronto breakwater.

At 8:06 p.m. pandemonium broke loose and hands reached for the incoherent teenager. She moaned, "No, mustn't touch me until I reach the breakwater. You'll disqualify me!" While excited voices reassured her that she *had* crossed the finish, they pulled the limp body from the water. Sirens wailed and 250,000 fans mobbed the girl as she was bundled in blankets and rushed to a nearby hotel.

Marilyn Bell had become the first swimmer in history to conquer the 32-mile stretch of Lake Ontario. Since she had been swept off course by the currents, she actually swam 42 miles in 21 hours. Millions of listeners had followed the hour-by-hour reports of her progress on the radio throughout the day while Toronto experi-enced its worst traffic jam in history, with hundreds of thousands of fans heading for the Exhibition. The response to Marilyn's swim was similar to Lindbergh's historic flight. Hearing that she was ineligible for the $10,000 prize offered only to Chadwick, admirers sent in gifts, eventually filling an entire warehouse. Meanwhile the C.N.E. officials, embarrassed over the turn of events, quickly offered the $10,000 reward to Marilyn.

The 17-year-old Canadian made every sports headline in the western world that day and eventually collected over $50,000 in cash and gifts, including three cars, three dogs, a year's supply of vitamins, breakfast food, cameras, clothes, a television set, two chinchillas worth $1,000 each, and a diamond maple-leaf brooch awarded by the city. It was even rumored that she would not have to pay taxes on her fortune

since she had competed for the "honor of Canada."

By the end of the week Marilyn was pro-nounced by her doctor to be healthy but slightly confused. Canadians, self-conscious of the youthfulness of their nation, were ecstatic over her new contribution to international sports. Thousands of letters poured in each day for their new heroine and included congratula-tions from the Prime Minister. That week Toronto held a ticker-tape parade which at-tracted a larger crowd than had gathered to greet Queen Elizabeth in 1951.

Marilyn Bell received offers of personal appearances and screen tests after her historic swim but finally decided to return to school instead. The "Lady of the Lake" had christened a new decade of marathon swimming.

The following year in August the entire inci-dent was almost repeated. An expectant crowd of 50,000 lined the Toronto waterfront to await a 19-year-old receptionist, named Shirley Campbell, who was attempting her first solo crossing of the lake. A Canadian newspaper, *The Telegram*, had convinced the teenager to try the swim even though she had only intended to practice for the upcoming Canadian Nation-al Exhibition $25,000 Cross-the-Lake Marathon on September 5.

Conditions could not have been more ideal since the lake registered 76°F. (24.5°C.) and was smooth and docile the day of her attempt. Unfortunately, with a mere 2½ miles remaining in her grueling 32-mile swim, Shirley was pulled from the lake in tears.

In spite of her defeat, the tremendous size of the crowd awaiting her exemplified that a new era of marathon swimming had arrived. Canada, although a nation of only 15 million, was becoming a leading producer of distance swimmers.

25. Crocodile of the Nile: Abo-Heif

The likeable, boisterous Egyptian, Abdel-Latif Abo-Heif, has added color to countless marathon swims over the years. In addition to his great swimming expertise, Abo-Heif is known for his huge pre-race feasts.

Most professional swimmers, such as Horacio Iglesias and Herman Willemse, eat lightly prior to a race and merely nibble a little toast and jelly, washed down with coffee. The 240-pound Abo-Heif, on the other hand, enters the dining room a full 4 hours prior to the race in order to take his time consuming two whole roast chickens, a quart of orange juice, a quart of milk, and an assortment of protein-rich foods. If he is not hungry, he simply does not eat anything, unlike other athletes who force themselves to eat and later vomit.

This pre-race orgy allows the Egyptian to swim the first 3 hours of a marathon without stopping for food. If he does not eat prior to race time, he must stop after only 20 minutes of swimming. Abo-Heif also has an astounding capability of eating heavily during a race. Once in a team marathon when he was replaced by his partner, Abo-Heif proceeded to consume two hamburgers, three fried eggs, and six glasses of orange soda. Rejuvenated and refueled, he got back in the water and led his team to a fourth-place finish.

The lovable Abo-Heif is also known as a great prankster. A favorite trick of his is to carry an open carton of apples to his escort boat before a race. Of course, he does not touch a single one, but the novices, believing they have

learned a trade secret, fuel up with apples and suffer stomach cramps throughout the race.

The 5-foot-10-inch broad-shouldered champion was born in 1929 to a retired schoolteacher and a member of the Egyptian Parliament. Abo-Heif had 14 brothers and sisters. At 17, he was sent to England to spend one year at Eton and then to graduate from Sandhurst Military Academy.

Abo-Heif then served in the Egyptian army, rising to the rank of colonel. Eventually he became the world's professional swimming champion three times and married a beautiful Greek opera singer. A national hero in Egypt, he plays the piano and speaks six languages.

In his native country Abo-Heif is always pursued by autograph hounds and continually makes newspaper headlines for his racing accomplishments. At the age of 26, the handsome, muscular Egyptian won his first professional event, the 1955 English Channel race.

His greatest year, however, was 1963 when he captured first place in the Capri-Naples Swim, winning $1,200, and came in second in the Atlantic City Marathon, winning $2,000. One week later he placed second in the 19-mile Lake St. John classic in Canada.

The 1963 Canadian National Exhibition race, however, was the most thrilling event that year. The prestigious 15-mile marathon offered $6,000 to the winner. The water temperature was a chilling 55°F. (12.8°C.), adding another dimension to the unpredictable event.

The Flying Dutchman, Herman Willemse,

Despite just having become the first man ever to complete the 60-mile Lake Michigan race in 1963, Abdel-Latif Abo-Heif still has plenty of energy left to face the barrage of questions thrown at him by members of the press.

took the lead, followed by the two great female competitors, Greta Andersen and Marty Sinn. The Canadian champion, Cliff Lumsden, swam next to Abo-Heif early in the race, but the Egyptian soon picked up his pace, leaving Cliff behind. Abo-Heif then passed Greta at the 5-mile mark, and she decided to drop out of the race. He then caught up to Marty Sinn (see page 107) who refused to relinquish her position. The two fought shoulder to shoulder until they pulled even with Willemse at the 14-mile point. At this time Abo-Heif surged ahead of Marty and crossed the finish a mere 2 minutes 15 seconds ahead of her. Marty completed the thrilling event 7 minutes 10 seconds ahead of the third-place winner, Willemse. The swimmers had maintained an exhausting pace with Abo-Heif finishing in a time of 7 hours 37 minutes 26 seconds.

This race was the climax and final one of the 1963 swimming season for all of the swimmers except the tireless Egyptian. Only 3 days later Abo-Heif entered the longest open-water swim in history, the 60-mile Lake Michigan Race (page 83). After enduring 35 hours of neck-and-neck competition, Abo-Heif collected the $15,000 first prize. At the age of 34 he had become the first man in history to complete the 60-mile open-water swim and set a record which has yet to be broken.

In 1969, when 40 years old, Abo-Heif won the 23-mile Chicoutimi (Quebec) race. Two years later he placed second in the 26-mile Guaymas, Mexico, classic. If and when the great swimmer ever retires, his unfaltering sense of humor, boisterousness, and amiability will be greatly missed in marathon swimming circles.

26. Marty Sinn

By the time she was 20, Mary Martha Sinn, nicknamed Marty, was one of the best distance swimmers in the world. The 5-foot-4-inch, 128-pound blond did not take her unusual sport too seriously, however, and once commented that it was silly to dive in and swim away with a crowd watching her as if she were in a zoo.

Marty grew up in Ann Arbor, Michigan, and learned to swim by sneaking into local swimming pools whenever she could. From the age of 11, she spent her summers as a camper and then a counselor at a swimming camp in central Ontario, Canada. Camp Ak-O-Mak's motto was "Lady, if you want your daughter to sew beads on a belt, send her somewhere else." Apparently, Marty learned something there, for by the time she was 14, she already held several state free-style records.

One of Marty's favorite pastimes at camp was swimming to town while her friends paddled there in canoes. When she learned about the 15-mile Canadian National Exhibition race, she thought it sounded easy, like swimming to town for ice cream.

In 1962, Marty needed money for college and decided to turn professional. Her first race was a 2-mile event in Kearney, Ontario. She won $25 and used the prize to pay for a trip to the C.N.E. race later that year. In that marathon she beat two female champions, placed fifth overall, and collected $2,300.

In 1963, she won $6,400 in an icy 15-mile event in Lake Ontario in which the water temperature dropped to 46°F. (7.7°C.) at one point. A total of 29 of the original 38 starters quit, and Marty suffered through hallucinations and severe depression. Although she fainted at the finish line, she managed to place second only 50 yards behind the winner. By the end of 1963, the beautiful Marty, art major at the University of Michigan, had competed in five races and finished first among the women in four of them.

While in college, Marty worked as an assistant swimming coach at an Ann Arbor Swim Club in order to have pool facilities at her disposal. She only took swimming seriously, however, 3 months out of the year, and many of her college friends did not even know about her victories. Distance swimming had begun as a lark for Marty, but during her college years had become an obligation. The long, lonely periods of swimming laps were tolerable at 14, but at 20 she wanted to explore new horizons.

Her attitudes and training methods differed greatly from most athletes. During the winter, Marty played handball with her boy friends, lifted 20-pound weights, and swam only an hour each day. During the summer she worked out 4 to 7 miles daily in the water but participated in cross-country running, a combination most coaches claim is incompatible. Her pre-race diet was highly unconventional also, since she gorged herself on chocolate ice cream, pancakes, and cake. She even attended parties before races.

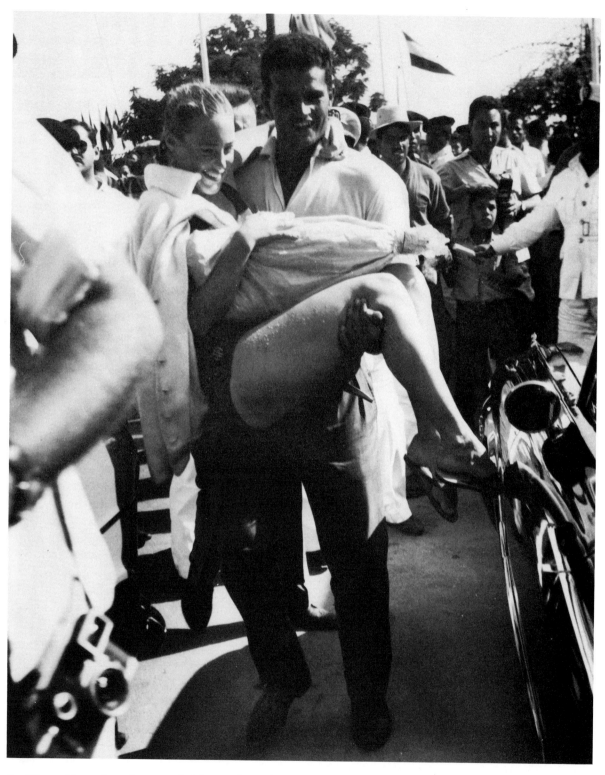

Smiling, though exhausted, Marty Sinn is carried to a waiting limousine which will take her to a hospital following a Suez Canal marathon swim in 1963.

In the 1963 Atlantic City Marathon, Marty tried another unusual racing tactic, that of swimming nude. The last 14 miles of that race were in a narrow, shallow strait between the island and the mainland. It was in this area that Marty and another competitor, John LaCoursiere of Montreal, swam side by side for several miles in the nude. As they passed under the bridges loaded with spectators, shouts of "Here come Adam and Eve" could be heard.

LaCoursiere, like Marty, was a somewhat unconventional swimmer and was known for his belief in post-hypnotic suggestion. In each race his coach repeated a key word at the critical moment, and this allegedly unleashed hidden reserves of energy.

In 1964, Marty again raced in the Atlantic City Marathon, but this time kept her suit on to avoid criticism and sunburn. Sunburn had been the least of the hazards in the race the previous year. Many swimmers sustained broken teeth and cut fingers while attempting to pull themselves along the pilings to fight the 5-knot tides.

Tricks were commonplace in the Atlantic City races, and some contestants were outright suspect. In a Suez Canal marathon in 1963 Marty noticed that she passed the same girl twice in three hours. Apparently, Marty had gone in a circle because Herman Willemse, the best distance swimmer in the world at the time, shouted to Marty, "They (the Egyptian escort crew) have been leading me in bloody circles!" Needless to say, the Egyptians won by a wide margin.

Greta Andersen in the 1959 Capri-Naples race witnessed a swimmer going by eating a banana. She did a double-take and observed that his other hand was holding a rope attached to his escort boat.

The 1964 Atlantic City Marathon was to be held on July 21 and offered $11,000 in cash prizes. Marty arrived 4 days prior to the race to meet her rower, Boomer Blair, and her feeder, Dr. Wilmer Abbott. Boomer was the captain of the Atlantic City lifeguards, had won the South Jersey lifeboat rowing championship nine times, and had rowed singlehandedly in every Atlantic City Marathon. Dr. Abbott, a dentist, had been the captain of the 1947 University of Pennsylvania swim team.

In addition to meeting her crew, Marty spent her few days prior to the race swimming and reading. Somewhat of an intellectual, Marty read voraciously. She also wondered why she was entering the race at all since near the end of June she had announced her retirement, and then again in July she had done the same. Marty was temperamental and not overly enthusiastic about swimming, since she believed there was too little financial gain to compensate for the agony of a marathon swim. Her main stimulus for swimming well was looking good to other professional swimmers. Public recognition was too far removed from the race itself.

On the morning of the race Marty awoke at 5 and was at the marina by 7:30. She greeted some of the other swimmers and then curled up on a boat for a nap. The international potpourri of swimmers consisted of five Americans, four Canadians, three Argentineans, one Yugoslav, one West German, one Netherlander, one Mexican, and three Egyptians subsidized by their government. Four of the competitors were women: Marty, Greta Andersen, and two unknowns. Marty, somewhat seasick, entered the back bay in eleventh place and suddenly felt rejuvenated by the calm water. She began singing an old Beatles' song to herself and had fun "picking off the boys" as she said later. She crossed the finish in seventh place, 19 minutes behind the leader, and collected $1,000.

Although pleased with her excellent showing (she finished first among the women), she still was not very enthusiastic about the sport. She once commented, "Marathon swimming is a tiny sport that's just kind of there, like mountain climbing." Whenever bored with it, Marty simply quits, saying, "None of this loneliness of the long-distance swimmer for me."

27. Manhattan Island Swim

Manhattan Island, the heart of New York City, has long been a favorite site for solo distance swimming due to its close proximity to the press. Unfortunately, to swim around the 28-mile coastline involves passing through two very polluted rivers and a bay as well as facing possibly the heaviest marine traffic in the world.

In the summer of 1915, Robert W. Dowling planned to do just that. As a young teenager he had trained at the New York Athletic Club and won many of their short amateur races. At the age of 17, he competed in a 2-mile race from the Battery at the foot of Manhattan Island to Sandy Hook. Having placed sixth in that event, Dowling decided to attempt to swim the 28 miles around the island the following summer (1915).

His father, an official with the Amateur Athletic Union, agreed to act as his coach. The experts warned him that the water would be too cold and the currents too strong, but he stuck by his son anyway.

On August 15, at 8:55 a.m. Robert dove from the Battery and headed up into the Hudson River. By riding the flood tide of the Atlantic Ocean, he swam an astounding 2 miles per hour. By noon he was swimming parallel to Central Park and by 2 p.m. Dowling had reached turbulent Spuyten Duyvil, the northern entrance to the Harlem River. In a mere 5 hours he had conquered the length of Manhattan Island, 12 miles. Now all he had to do was enter the calm Harlem River, swim east for 1 mile and then merely ride down the currents of the Harlem and East Rivers.

As Robert reached Spuyten Duyvil, however, the tide turned decisively. The ebb tide took control causing the Hudson to flow with a 3-mile-per-hour force against him. If Dowling had reached the entrance an hour earlier, he would have gotten around the corner into the Harlem River easily. Instead the current pushed him away from the entrance, forcing him to head back to the Battery.

Dowling plodded on for 3 hours. If he could reach the starting point, he could have at least claimed to have gone an equivalent distance, but at 5:30 p.m. he was dragged onto his escort boat. He had been in the water $8\frac{1}{2}$ hours and had conquered $18\frac{1}{2}$ miles but was disillusioned with his first try. Back in the boat, however, the teenager immediately began planning a September attempt, vowing to use charts and tide tables this time.

On Sunday, September 5, at 8:30 a.m. Robert dove into the water at 225th Street at the western end of the Harlem River and headed for the nearby Hudson entrance at Spuyten Duyvil. This time he was circling in the opposite direction. With the current's help he swam at over 3 miles per hour, reaching the Battery by 1 p.m. In spite of motor boats littering his path, Dowling covered the 12 miles down the Hudson in only $4\frac{1}{2}$ hours. The free ride ended, however, when Robert took a full hour to cover the mile from the Battery up the East River to the Brooklyn Bridge.

For the next 4 hours the currents again turned in his favor. At 6:15 p.m. the entrance from the East River to the Harlem River came

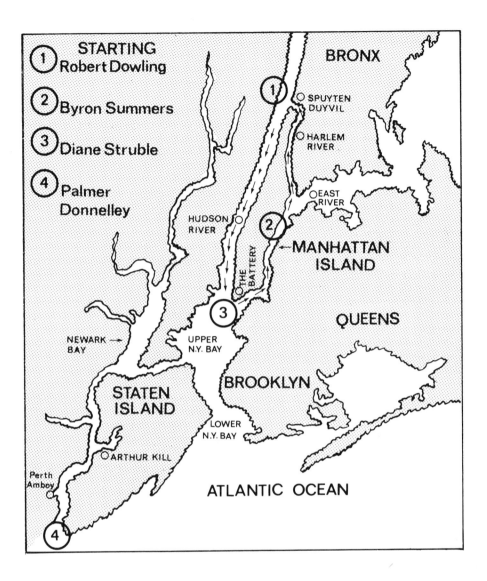

The map labels:

STARTING
1 Robert Dowling
2 Byron Summers
3 Diane Struble
4 Palmer Donnelley

BRONX
SPUYTEN DUYVIL
HARLEM RIVER
EAST RIVER
HUDSON RIVER
THE BATTERY
MANHATTAN ISLAND
QUEENS
NEWARK BAY
UPPER N.Y. BAY
STATEN ISLAND
BROOKLYN
LOWER N.Y. BAY
ARTHUR KILL
Perth Amboy
ATLANTIC OCEAN

into view indicating that the boy had covered 8¼ miles in a brief 4 hours. From that point on Dowling became increasingly exhausted, and it took a trying 3½ hours to cover the 3 miles in the Harlem River to the 181st Street Washington Bridge. As darkness fell on the lone swimmer, the lights on the escort boat marked his path.

In the final mile of the 28-mile swim, Dowling could hear boat horns at the finish line cheering him home. At 10:15 p.m. after 13 hours 45 minutes in the water, Robert embarrassed the officials who claimed it could not be done by becoming the first person in history to swim around Manhattan Island.

The following year Ida Elionsky broke Dowling's record by completing the swim in 11 hours 35 minutes, a time which was to remain unbroken for 11 years. Byron Summers, a California college student, set the new record in 1927 by using nautical charts and tide tables. He also commandeered an excellent escort crew from the 89th Street Volunteer Life Saving Station.

Summers' plan was to begin the swim at the

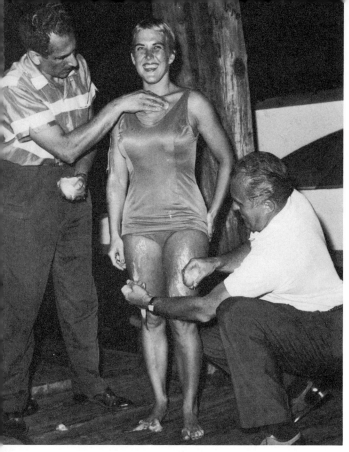

Diane Struble smiles confidently as she gets a coat of grease before plunging into the heavily polluted waters at the Battery. The 25-year-old mother of three didn't even stop when she had completed the 28-mile circuit—she started on a second round trip!

89th Street station by sprinting northward. If he could maintain a fast pace, he would get the toughest 7½ miles out of the way first. Then after these first 3 hours, he would ride down the Hudson, arriving at the Battery in 4 or 5 hours. Byron Summers completed his swim in an astounding 8 hours 56 minutes by averaging 3 miles per hour with the tides.

Over the years, freighters became the swimmer's greatest hazard on this circuit. Eventually the ships' captains complained so much that City Hall outlawed swimming in the shipping lanes without special permission. In 1959, permission was granted since New York was celebrating the 350th anniversary of the Dutch exploration of the Hudson River. The Schaeffer Brewing Co. contracted with 25-year-old Diane Struble to swim around Manhattan Island that year as part of the celebration. The previous year she had become the first person in history to swim the 32-mile-long Lake George in up-state New York. By swimming for 35 hours during that conquest, she had set a record for immersion.

On August 15, with the City Council's approval, Diane dove from the sea wall at the Battery and started up the East River. To the delight of newsmen and television cameramen, the 5-foot-3-inch, 138-pound girl swam within 100 yards of shore during the entire swim. After 11 hours 21 minutes, a cheering crowd of 500 admirers greeted Diane at the finish. The young swimmer, however, was determined to circle the island a second time and did not stop swimming until two lifeguards hauled her out of the water.

In 1961, in spite of heavy industrial pollution, a 21-year-old lifeguard named Palmer Donnelley attempted to circle Staten Island. He dove in from Perth Amboy, New Jersey, at 5:47 p.m. and headed up Arthur Kill Straits. During the afternoon of the next day he encountered unfavorable tides and was forced to wait for them to change. Eventually that evening the exhausted lifeguard reached the finish and was whisked away in an ambulance. He later collected $2,000 from a local newspaper and civic leaders for completing the 35-mile feat in 25 hours.

28. Daring Diana

As of July 25, 1970, pretty, 22-year-old Diana Nyad had never seen a marathon swim, had never raced in open water, and had never raced farther than 1,500 meters. By the end of the following day she had captured the title, "best woman distance swimmer in the world."

On July 26, Diana stood on a beach at Lake Ontario among 20 of the best marathon swimmers in the world. A gun was about to be fired marking the start of Labatt's International Ten-Mile Marathon Swim. Diana was scared to death and her fears were only compounded by the presence of Judith DeNys, the best female distance swimmer in the world in the 1960's. Judith was loudly proclaiming that if any woman ever beat her, she would retire. Then as if sensing the strength of the opposition, she brazenly approached Diana to say, "You're not going to beat me."

As the gun fired, novices and veterans alike ran to the water and dove in. Abo-Heif and another Egyptian swam extremely close to Diana throughout the race. She eventually pulled away from them and crossed the finish in a time of 4 hours 23 minutes. In her first distance race, she set a women's world record for 10 miles and collected $400 for being the first female to finish. Judith DeNys kept her promise and retired after being beaten by Diana.

That same year Nyad entered the unpredictable Chicoutimi, Quebec, 28-mile marathon. In the 1969 race 22 of the world's greatest swimmers started and none finished. This year,

1970, almost all of the escort boats were lost in a violent storm the night before the race, and replacements were not commandeered until hours after the start. The course included 18 miles of the Saguenay River, 2 or 3 miles along a rocky shoreline boasting dangerous riptides, and then 7 miles into a large bay called Ha! Ha! Bay, known for its unpredictable tides.

As Diana stood on the shoreline at Chicoutimi awaiting the starting gun, she wondered what she was doing there confronted with a treacherous 28-mile swim when all she had ever attempted previously was 10 miles!

The gun was fired, and Diana dove in without benefit of goggles or escort boat. Only a few miles out she became disoriented and nearly hit shore. She managed to redirect herself and continued on unguided for $4\frac{1}{2}$ hours. At this point, 14 miles down river from the start, her coach finally caught up to her in a new boat. Although she had not had any food during the long swim, she surprisingly was in second place behind Argentina's Horacio Iglesias. Her coach fed her hot chocolate and aspirin as soon as he located her.

Diana was a full 2 miles in front of the third place competitor but made a costly mistake. Instead of entering the bay along the rocky shoreline, she chose to enter the dangerous riptides instead. Only 6 miles from the finish at Bagotville, she ended up swimming for an hour on a tidal treadmill leading nowhere. The tide was not to change for hours and if she had stopped swimming, Diana would have been swept out into the Atlantic Ocean.

Eventually the other competitors caught up to her, saw her predicament, and wisely chose the rocky route into the bay. After 9 hours, Diana's coach knew it was useless to go on and pulled the furious swimmer into the boat.

The Argentinean, Iglesias, was having even more serious problems. At the 27-mile point with only a mile remaining in the race, he was hauled unconscious from the water, rushed to a nearby hospital, and fed intravenously for 3 hours. In this ill-fated race, only three of the original 22 swimmers managed to complete the event.

Diana Nyad had been born Diana Sneed, but when she was 3 her mother was divorced, then briefly married to a wealthy Greek land developer, Aristotle Zason Nyad. It seems appropriate that Diana took his last name, for Webster defined "Naiad" as "one of the nymphs in ancient mythology, living in and giving life to lakes, rivers, springs, and fountains."

When Diana's mother divorced again, the 12-year-old found a father figure in her future coach, Jack Nelson. She was at an impressionable age, and a friendship developed which was to last many years.

In the ninth grade the determined youngster entered the Florida senior regional championships and finished second in the 200-meter backstroke, only 0.2 seconds behind the winner. She went on to win at several state meets but never did better than twelfth in national events. She worked extremely hard and had her heart set on the Olympics. Even today she claims that she would trade all of her awards for an Olympic gold medal.

At the age of 16, however, Diana suffered a severe setback. She came down with endocarditis, a viral infection of the heart. That summer she was confined to bed and not allowed any visitors, but by fall Diana began swimming again. This time, however, to her horror she found that she was much slower than previously. Heartbroken, she realized that all of her years of intensive training would not get her to Mexico City and the Olympics.

Her coach reassured her that some day she would be great at something, since already she was a great human being. Diana graduated from high school and immediately entered Emory University as a pre-med student. The ambitious teenager was determined to become a surgeon but also to continue her swimming.

Diana's freshman year was not typical of the studious pre-med student. After an evening at the library she threw on her running clothes and ran laps around the dark, deserted track. In the mornings she would swim from 5:30 to 7:30 and arrive at her classes with wet hair. For some reason the dean of women at Emory took an immediate dislike to Diana and claimed that the girl was merely trying to attract attention to herself.

Diana, like most spunky freshmen, was in on many campus pranks. One day an announcement circulated that someone was going to jump with a parachute into the courtyard between the women's dorms. Diana bought a parachute, boots, and jump suit and at the appointed hour appeared on the fourth floor of the dorm. A large crowd gathered below as others peered from windows. Unfortunately, the school's deans were also present.

Daring Diana was scared to death, knowing that the parachute was not folded right and that obviously it could not open within four floors. She fluffed up the air pockets anyway and leaped from the building to everyone's amazement. Fortunately, Diana merely bruised her heel bones, but within a few days much greater problems were to arise. She soon received a message from the dean demanding that she come to her office. When Diana appeared, the school official briskly told her that it was obvious that she wanted to kill herself.

Late one night soon after the incident, Diana played a game called Hangman with a friend. This is a well-known word game which involves drawing stick figures of hanged men.

Unfortunately, they drew on a formica table with a felt-tipped pen, and the ink did not wash off the table. This was reported to the dean who called Diana to her office and slyly commented that it was strange for anyone to be drawing pictures of hanged men at 3 a.m.

The shocked teenager felt as if she were in a bad dream where everyone thought she was crazy. Furious at the accusation, Diana shouted, "My God, haven't you ever played the Hangman game?" The dean jumped back from her desk, apparently afraid that the girl was going to attack her. A few days later, the hurt and misunderstood student was asked to leave the university.

Bewildered, she set off across the country, exploring and writing as therapy to ease her mind. She worked for a while as a lifeguard in Fort Lauderdale, and in the spring mailed off applications to Yale, Michigan, and Stanford. Unfortunately, a letter from the dean accompanied her transcripts from Emory, and she was rejected by all three schools.

Diana traveled to Europe for a month and a half, and when she returned home, a friend suggested that she apply to Lake Forest College in Illinois. On New Year's Day 1970, Daring Diana called the admissions director, explained her predicament, and read him the letter the dean would send. Two days later she was accepted.

The director of financial aid, Gordon White, and the school's swimming coach, Karl Sutter, both had heard of Diana through her old friend and coach, Jack Nelson. They each thought she deserved another chance, so they gave it to her.

Diana did not let them down either. In the next five semesters she managed four straight A averages and one A minus. She also played on the Lake Forest varsity tennis team, and spent two nights a week taking drama classes in Chicago, an hour's train ride from school.

Diana yearned to study something creative as opposed to the dull memory work needed for medicine. Therefore, she switched majors from pre-med to drama. On top of all her academic activities and tennis matches, the amazing girl continued swimming. She entered championship meets but never was able to regain the speed she had prior to her bout with heart disease. Coach Sutter was impressed with Diana's unfaltering mental toughness and determination and decided she had potential as a distance swimmer rather than a sprinter.

During the hectic winter and spring semesters Diana averaged less than 4 hours of sleep a night. In addition, once each week she stayed awake the entire night writing a paper on 19th-century French literature. Juggling all of her activities was hard work, but she kept each in its proper perspective with studies always coming first and social life taking a back seat.

The 1971 Canadian marathon season opened with the arduous Chicoutimi, Quebec, race. This year there were 30 entrants, including Diana. Throughout the race Diana felt she was out of shape, and by the 20-mile point she knew she would have to use everything she had. At this point the 1970 world champion dropped out due to leg cramps, and the Argentinean, Horacio Iglesias, was only 300 yards in front of Diana. Within the next 2 miles Diana took over the lead in what was only the third marathon in her life.

Her lead was short-lived, however, and going into the final half mile sprint, she had fallen back to fifth place. A crowd of 20,000 awaited her at the finish, but she lost more ground and came in seventh in a time of 8 hours 46 minutes. Diana placed well, however, considering that only 10 of the original 30 starters completed the event, labeled one of the world's toughest races.

Only a week later the 24-Hour La Tuque Swim was to be held (see page 88). This team event started at 3 p.m. Saturday and ran until 3 p.m. Sunday in Lake Louie. More than 35,000 French Canadians invaded the tiny town in Quebec that year to witness the race.

Most of the contestants swam alternating

3-lap stints and rested in between. Diana and her teammate, Guston Paré, only swam one lap at a time. The tireless girl averaged 7 minutes 21 seconds a lap and set a new women's record for the event. In 24 hours the two of them covered 54 miles and finished the race in third place. Diana, however, had not worn goggles throughout the ordeal and unknowingly suffered from a hemorrhaging eye. At the end of the race she was rushed unconscious to a hospital where they injected glucose intravenously.

In a press conference later that day the great Abo-Heif announced that Diana had the stuff of a champion. She was pleased that finally she had earned the respect of her fellow swimmers. This was almost more important to the young girl than winning.

The superwoman graduated from Lake Forest College, Phi Beta Kappa, and entered New York University to pursue a PhD in comparative literature. In 1974, Daring Diana attempted the first double crossing of Lake Ontario. She became the first person ever to swim the 32-mile stretch of lake from north to south against the current of the Niagara River, and did it in 18 hours 20 minutes. After a brief 15-minute rest, she regreased, spoke to the press, and plunged back in for the return trip. Within 2 hours she was hauled unconscious from the lake.

Diana has grown bitter over the lack of public recognition given to distance swimmers. An immense amount of training and hard work go into the sport, and she claims that she has put more strenuous hours into it than tennis player Jimmy Connors will know in a lifetime. At the age of 25 she could do a thousand sit-ups and yet never did them on a regular basis. She ran the mile in 5:15 and had a lung capacity which was greater than many football players. Her heartbeat was 47 beats per minute compared to the average athlete's 60 plus beats per minute. Diana justly claimed that these characteristics were due to hard work rather than genetics.

When asked why she swam in the torturous marathons, she replied, "For glory and money. To *be* someone." She seemed to be in a perpetual race to test her own limits and capabilities. In addition, Diana enjoyed the sense of camaraderie which develops among professional swimmers. Prior to a race each competitor shares the same anxiety and tension, and during the event they each must battle the same water conditions, temperatures, and aches and pains.

Each swimmer has to dig deep to find the mental fortitude to keep going after 12 or more hours in the water. Usually a swimmer's blood sugar drops drastically and severe depression sets in. Each hour during a race, Diana drinks a cup of hot powdered liquid containing 1,300 calories and more protein per tablespoon than an 8-ounce steak. Before an event she loads up on five or six raw eggs, cereal, toast, jelly, and juice.

Nyad, however, believes that 80 per cent of the success in a race is mental. The sense of isolation can be overwhelming, since a swimmer is totally cut off from communication. The goggles are generally foggy, making the athlete virtually blind, and the waves lapping against the bathing cap make the swimmer deaf as well. The head is turned with every stroke, and the arms are lifted about 60 times each minute, hour after hour. Research has shown that a person floating in a tank with eyes and ears covered becomes disoriented and dazed. He is lulled into the dream state which distance swimmers claim is typical in long events.

The only problem, according to Diana, which cannot be overcome with mental fortitude is cold. Her worst experience with this was during a training swim prior to the Capri-Naples race in 1974. On the day she was to leave for Europe, Nyad decided to go for a one hour warm-up swim in Lake Ontario. She paddled an easy 1,000 strokes out into the lake and turned around to get a sighting on shore. Suddenly, Diana realized that she could not feel her legs and could not even lift them to the surface. She tried to scream for help, but her breath stuck in her throat. She attempted a slow breaststroke but was unable to close her fingers. Finally, someone on the beach noticed that she was in trouble and just barely clinging to some shallow rocks. The man waded out to her and carried her to shore. His hands, however, at a normal 98.6°F. (37°C.) burned her chilled, bright-red skin. Nyad was rushed to a hospital and placed in a warmer. She went to Europe, but suffered from severe burns throughout the Capri-Naples race.

In October, 1975, Diana attempted to break a 48-year-old record by completing the perilous 28-mile swim around Manhattan Island. When asked, "Why Manhattan?" Nyad replied, "The world is four-fifths water, but the point is to swim where the people are." She failed in her first attempt due to Hurricane Eloise. She chose to enter the water at East 89th Street as had Byron Summers nearly 50 years earlier (see page 110). Then, swimming through one of the world's busiest harbors, surrounded by huge ferryboats and tugboats, she reached the Battery at the southern tip of the island at dusk. Diana bravely swam into the night through rain, wind, pollution, and traffic but was halted by a powerful tidal current. For an hour she made no progress at all and grew exhausted and incoherent. Finally, someone mercifully pulled her from the slime and put her in a police boat. Gray and barely alive, Nyad was rushed to a hospital with a flood of reporters in hot pursuit. Only an hour later she began talking about "next time."

By the time she made her second attempt, Diana had thoroughly researched the maze of tides and river currents. The city certainly did not encourage her, and this made obtaining information difficult. She decided to start in the East River at 89th Street near the treacherous Hell Gate at slack tide before it turned upstream. From there she would have a brief swim up the East River, north into the Harlem River, and down the Hudson. This route would allow her to follow the tide most of the way.

In preparing for the swim, Diana spoke with a man who had tried it in 1961. He swam for more than 19 hours and at one point was sucked under by a whirlpool and could not surface for 400 yards. Nyad was not deterred by this story or by the fact that she had vomited for 3 days after her first attempt.

Cliff Lumsden, the Canadian swimmer, had acted as Diana's coach during the first swim, but was unable to return to New York for the second try. Her other coach, Sue Wiersum, simply refused and told Diana she was being masochistic. The adrenaline was flowing, however, and the determined swimmer felt she "had to *do* something now!"

The positive side to failure in an endurance event is that it generates interest. Nyad's first attempt received little pre-race publicity, but her second one had all of New York watching. The sea wall at 89th Street was overflowing with reporters, film crews, and television cameras. To the often repeated question, "Why?" Diana merely replied that she had an intimate psychological relationship with marathon swimming.

At 11:35 a.m. the 25-year-old grad student entered the water across from the mouth of Flushing Creek. An apt name, for Diana was soon swimming past dead rats, birds, and decaying trash. Her goggles quickly became clouded over with scum. She swam on in spite of the garbage and even managed feedings of Sustagen and dextrose. The Hudson River, although a warm 65°F. (18.3°C.), was unusually rough. Nyad did not seem to mind, however, and swam well. At one point a friend, temporarily put into action as coach of the day, held up a sign saying, "Looking strong. We love you."

An hour later he suddenly flashed another message reading, "Slow down," since it was only 4 p.m. and Diana was almost to the Battery. The tide would not favor her until 5 p.m. Her amateur crew worried and was

New York University graduate student Diana Nyad slips into the waters of the East River off 89th Street on her way to a record-breaking swim around Manhattan in 1975.

convinced she would fail again. Diana, however, removed her goggles and gently backstroked and drifted to Battery Park. She looked up now and for the first time saw people on the banks cheering her on.

At 5:05 p.m. Nyad made it around the Battery, and the current flowing out from the East River stopped. She swam beneath the Brooklyn Bridge and watched the sun set over Wall Street. The novice crew gradually relaxed, and Diana continued on past the United Nations Building. She finally completed her historic swim in a record-breaking 7 hours 57 minutes, and this time there was a crowd of admiring spectators shouting congratulations as she left the water.

Having apparently avoided hepatitis, typhoid, and dysentery, Diana awoke the next morning at the usual hour, downed two raw eggs, and ran 3 miles to Barnard College where she coached swimming. At noon, she ate her usual meal of raw meat and raw vegetables and then went to N.Y.U. for class. Between 3 and 5 p.m. she played squash as she did every day with the hope of someday dominating that field as she had marathon swimming for 6 years.

Her plans for the immediate future, however, were to swim each of the Great Lakes. Her swim around Manhattan Island attracted the attention she had hoped for since soon afterward she made several television appearances, worked on a documentary, and was interviewed for a sports announcing job. In addition, a publishing company asked her to write a book, and an agent promised her up to $75,000 per year in endorsements, a figure five times the amount she had earned in her entire swimming career.

29. Lynne Cox's Catalina and Cook's Strait Swims

Stocky, ambitious Lynne Cox is neither swift nor stylish nor competitive and yet, up until August of 1976 she was the fastest swimmer of the English Channel in history. At the age of 15, the California high school student first attempted the swim in July, 1972, and set a record in 9 hours 57 minutes. Although this shattered the previous record by 26 minutes, it only lasted 3 weeks! An American swimmer, Davis Hart, bettered Lynne's time by 13 minutes. Not to be outdone, Cox returned to England the following summer and set a new record by a woman for the crossing in a time of 9 hours 36 minutes. That record stood as the fastest women's Channel swim in history until broken on August 31, 1976, by Wendy Brooks, who swam from England to France in 8 hours 56 minutes, a time which also shattered the men's record of 9 hours 35 minutes.

Lynne comes from a family of swimmers, including her younger sisters Ruth and Laura who swim competitively and play water polo. Her older brother, Dave attends Brigham Young University on a swimming scholarship. Lynne's parents, Dr. and Mrs. Albert Cox, encouraged their ambitious youngsters and moved the entire family west to California from New Hampshire so that they could enjoy their sport year round. Lynne became interested in distance swimming when she found she was being beaten in shorter events by 10- and 11-year-old girls.

Late one night in September, 1974, Cox waded into the chilly water off Santa Catalina Island and struck out for Los Angeles, 21 miles away. Although she had successfully completed this swim at the age of 14, she now was attempting to break the world record for the event, set by her own brother.

The darkness became intimidating to the teenager and to make matters worse, a thick fog blanketed the ocean soon after her departure. The eeriness of the lonely sea was enhanced by the phosphorescent white caps, caused by the seasonal "red tide," made up of billions of one-celled plant-like animals.

The 55-foot escort boat was barely visible to the anxious swimmer, so she shouted that she wanted to talk to her parents. Dr. and Mrs. Cox immediately got into a small skiff and headed for their daughter to offer encouragement and reassurance. Only 500 yards away, however, the tiny boat became lost in the dense fog. The bewildered parents began to circle the area looking for Lynne, but it was 2 hours before they found her sobbing, disoriented, and terrifyingly alone.

Lynne's lack of confidence forced her out of the water that night, but her family and friends stuck by her, giving her the desire to try again. This time, however, her parents were to arrange everything and not tell her until the day of the swim.

Lynne returned to her routine, attending

Just before her first English Channel swim, 15-year-old Lynne Cox waves happily to the camera. Shortly after, she broke all previous records by 26 minutes.

the middle of a cold ocean in the dead of night. She tried not to think about sharks but grasped at any excuse to stop swimming. She sang songs to herself in an attempt to fight off the overpowering sense of boredom and isolation. About 7 miles from the island, white streaks flashed beneath Lynne. By this time she was so exhausted that she merely thought to herself, "Maybe the sharks will go after Mark on the paddleboard." Later she was informed that they were only porpoises.

At dawn Lynne was told that she had an hour left to better her brother's record for the Catalina swim. The teenager grinned and began a sustained sprint for the finish. When she finally touched the rocky island cliffs, Lynne learned that she had bettered her brother's record by just 2 minutes, although he had crossed the more conventional route from the island to the mainland.

Great athletes such as Lynne receive little or no financial reward for their accomplishments. In fact, Dr. and Mrs. Cox spent $6,000 financing just the two English Channel swims. In addition to travel expenses and motel bills during the weeks while they awaited suitable weather, they paid out $250 for a pilot and escort boat, $25 for a Channel Swimming Association observer, $14 for Association dues, and $40 for a world-record-holder plaque. All Lynne received in return was a watch awarded each year by the Association to the Channel swimmer with the fastest time.

In addition to the enormous expense involved, each athlete must research the tides, currents, and special problems of every swim by corresponding with universities, oceanographic institutions, and other swimmers. Lynne, however, does not devote all of her time and resources to swimming, for she also excels as a student at Los Alamitos High School.

In February, 1975, Lynne attempted one of the most difficult swims in the world, the $13\frac{1}{4}$-mile turbulent stretch of water between New Zealand's North and South Islands, known as

class in the morning and swimming 8 to 10 miles each afternoon at Long Beach. As she swam hour after hour between the jetties, her parents or her friend, Laura Rothwell, walked along the shore. A sympathetic Long Beach lifeguard, Mark Le Gault, paddled beside her on a surfboard whenever possible.

At noon on Sunday, September 23, Lynne's mother told her daughter that she was to attempt the Catalina Swim again that night. Mrs. Cox had arranged to accompany Lynne in a skiff and also to have someone next to the swimmer at all times on a paddleboard.

At 10:35 p.m. a gun was fired near the Marineland Pier in Los Angeles, and Lynne dove in, heading for Santa Catalina Island. Her pace was rapid at first in order to overcome the incoming tide. This time the night favored the young swimmer—Lynne could now see sparkling stars and a familiar golden moon watching over her.

Around midnight Lynne's anxieties surfaced again as she wondered what she was doing in

Cook's Strait. The tidal currents in this area are so powerful and unpredictable that it was 34 years after the first attempt before the strait was finally crossed. Since that time there have been about 20 attempts, and only two successful swims.

The topography of the area is dramatic. The island shores are mountainous, and the floor of the strait consists of steep peaks and troughs. Ocean currents are funneled between the islands with a violent velocity. Submarine currents, sweeping from the Antarctic through the submerged mountains and valleys, become dangerous whirlpools and eddies. On the surface of the churning sea, conditions are not much better. Like the currents, the wind too gathers force as it is funneled between the two islands.

The story of the first crossing of Cook's Strait comes from New Zealand's Maori tribesmen. They recount the tale of the ill-fated couple, Hine-poupou and her husband, Manini-pounamu, who lived on the South Island during the mid-1800's. The straying husband apparently fell in love with a younger woman and decided to do something about his predicament. He loaded his wife into a canoe, paddled across Cook's Strait to the North Island, and left her there while he returned to his girl. Meanwhile, Hine-poupou, raging mad, chanted to the gods for help, and dove into the turbulent strait to return to the South Island. As the story goes, she was led safely across the channel by several benevolent dolphins, but when she arrived, her husband was out fishing. Hine-poupou again pleaded with the gods until suddenly a violent storm arose over the strait. The unfaithful Manini-pounamu was never seen or heard from again.

Although 18-year-old Lynne Cox had never heard this story, she too was aided by dolphins in her adventurous crossing and believed that God had sent them. She also relied on more earthly assistance, namely a fisherman, John Cataldo, who had three years of experience in Cook's Strait. Cataldo, claiming to understand the capricious, deadly currents, served as a guide and pilot for two of the three previous successful attempts and also for most of the swims during the preceding 12 years.

Lynne prepared for her venture by swimming 5 to 15 miles each day. She then flew to New Zealand with John Sonnichsen, a marathon swimming coach and friend for many years. On the way they also picked up Sandra Blewett, a New Zealand distance swimmer, who had given Lynne the idea of attempting Cook's Strait. Sandra originally had intended to try the swim herself but had injured her back in the meantime. She sportingly agreed to assist Lynne instead.

On February 4, the tempting weather forecast called for 10- to 20-knot winds in the morning, then dropping to only 5 to 10 knots later in the day. The weather, however, like the currents was totally unpredictable, and Lynne was eventually confronted with 25-knot northerlies with 40-knot gusts.

At 3 a.m. Cataldo's escort boat, the San Antonio, headed for Ohau Point. Just before 8 a.m. Lynne entered the chilly, gray sea and struck out on her journey. Within minutes she was swallowed by the violent Terawhiti riptide, known for consuming small, unsuspecting boats. Lynne, however, wisely had a lifeguard on a paddleboard accompanying her, and he talked her through the vicious current.

Lynne maintained a rapid pace for the next $3\frac{1}{2}$ hours but was continually carried south of the predetermined route. The path through Cook's Strait is commonly a series of S's, and Lynne eventually changed direction seven times during her swim, once even going backwards.

Battling the powerful currents drained Cox mentally and physically. After $5\frac{1}{2}$ hours and with just more than half of the distance covered, Lynne swam to the boat and announced that she was quitting. In spite of Sonnichsen's booming protests and admonitions through his bullhorn, Lynne ripped off her cap and goggles signifying the end.

Sensing her role in the drama, Sandra

immediately plunged in and swam with her friend until Lynne had regained her rhythm and confidence. Finally, seasick and racked with pain Sandra was hauled back into the boat. Lynne, however, continued on accompanied by various lifeguards taking their turn on the paddleboard. Interspersed with Lynne's mentally low periods came encouragement from the outside world. First, a freighter pulled alongside and raised an American flag. Later Lynne was told about the flood of phone calls pouring into the Wellington radio station urging her to keep going.

This attention and praise was not enough stimulus, however, and after 2 more hours Lynne demanded to be pulled out of the ocean. Suddenly, as if reliving Hine-poupou's successful crossing, a dozen or more dolphins, dancing

Here's Lynne at 18, adjusting her cap as she prepares to begin her swim across Cook's Strait between the North and South Islands of New Zealand. She became the first woman to conquer the treacherous waters.

and squeaking gleefully, surfaced near Lynne. For the remaining 4 hours they swam in pairs or small groups around her and even dove over her.

With the dolphins at her side Lynne swam to within $1\frac{1}{4}$ miles of the South Island. Suddenly, the currents became so powerful that she could not progress at all. The winds grew violent while the towering clouds became ominous. A fishing boat scouting for currents warned the escort crew that a new current only 400 yards from shore headed away from Perano Head. Forced to change her route again, Lynne swam parallel to the coast and searched for a different landing location. Her crew realized, however, that she now risked swimming into the raging Tory Channel which flowed away from the island.

Fortunately, Lynne cleared this current as well as the outgoing tide within a half hour of the finish. As if the strait had conceded defeat, the wind suddenly died down, the sea became calm, and the dolphins disappeared.

Lynne was pulled gently into the bay by a new tide, and joyfully walked ashore to the chiming of church bells. Although ashen-faced and freezing, she smiled at the jubilant crowd of "Kiwis" (as New Zealanders call themselves) who greeted her back at the North Island that night. She even talked of possibly swimming the Irish Sea. Lynne thought about the dolphin escort and wondered if God had sent them.

Lynne Cox became the first woman to swim Cook's Strait, but missed breaking the record time by 2 hours $28\frac{1}{2}$ minutes. In spite of this she set a new standard for courage and perseverance by battling the 5-foot swells, 25-knot winds, fierce currents, sharks, and killer whales for an agonizing 12 hours.

In January, 1977, Lynne added another feather in her cap by being the first person ever to swim the turbulent Strait of Magellan between Chile and Tierra del Fuego.

30. Strait of Juan de Fuca Swim

One of the most difficult and dangerous swims in the world is the crossing of the frigid 18-mile channel between Vancouver Island and the state of Washington. Not only does the water average a frigid 48°F. (9°C.), but the island is lined with the deadly Race Rocks. The powerful ebb and flood tides literally race into this area making it a potential death trap for the unsuspecting swimmer.

In April, 1955 a newspaper, *The Victoria Times,* offered $1,000 for the first swimmer to successfully cross the infamous strait from Victoria, Canada, to the city of Port Angeles on the American shore. By early July four men and three women had tried but were stopped by overpowering tidal currents, choppy seas, and unbearable water temperatures. If they had waited until August, the water would have been warmer but the longer they stalled, the more they risked losing the prize to a more daring competitor.

A Tacoma, Washington, logger named Bert Thomas had determined the previous winter that he would cross the chilling strait. The 29-year-old ex-marine and frogman had trained by swimming in Puget Sound, but had already failed four times to cross the strait due to the cold. He finally realized that fat was essential for overcoming the brutal temperatures. Over the winter he downed gallons of milk, pounds of steak and potatoes, and eventually added 40 pounds to his 230-pound, 6-foot-2-inch frame.

In mid-July, 1955, Thomas decided he was ready, but this time he would attempt the crossing from the U.S. to Canada instead of the more conventional, reverse direction. He arrived at the harbor at Port Angeles and found an uninviting 48°F. (9°C.) sea, streaked with oil and sewage. The well-padded swimmer greased his body and donned a woman's bathing cap for added warmth.

At 6:50 p.m. Bert plunged in, timing his departure to coincide with the gentle evening ebb tide. For once the wind did not battle him, and the usual chop was replaced by gentle swells. Three escort boats assisted Bert, one scouting ahead for helpful currents and the others remaining by his side. In the first two hours he quickly covered a full 4 miles in spite of an hourly stop to refuel with orange juice and to smoke a cigarette.

By 11 p.m. Thomas was being carried safely away from the dangerous Race Rocks by the flood tide and at midnight had reached the halfway point. By 1 a.m. Bert and his crew could see the lights in Victoria that the towns-people had turned on for him. With this added incentive the tireless swimmer picked up his pace, covering the next 1½ miles in only 20 minutes. He jovially shouted to the boat, "You fellas got nothing to worry about. Sit back and relax."

By dawn the sight of the crowds on shore motivated Thomas to sprint the final 25 yards. After 11 hours and 17 minutes in the cold sea,

Ex-marine and frogman Bert Thomas put on an extra 40 pounds of fat to fend off the cold waters of the Juan de Fuca Strait. It must have helped, because on July 8, 1955, he became the first person to make it across the deadly 18-mile channel.

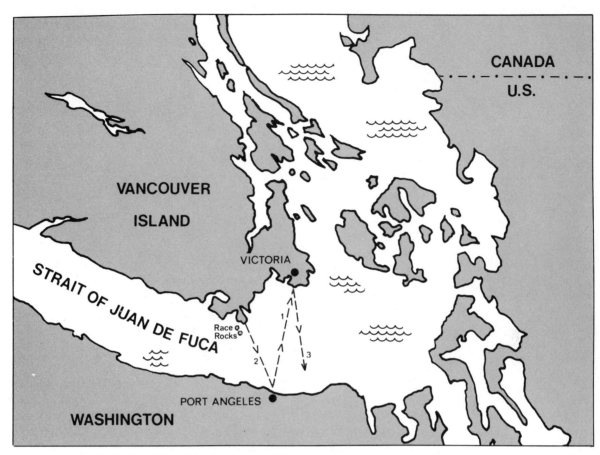

Strait of Juan de Fuca swim.

he staggered ashore and fell into his wife's arms becoming the first swimmer in history to conquer the Juan de Fuca Strait. Soon afterward an ambulance drove him downtown to collect his $1,000 prize. He later was given an additional $2,000 in bonuses and was heard to say that next he planned to try the Golden Gate swim and the Strait of Gibraltar.

In August, 1956, Marilyn Bell (see page 101) decided to attempt a crossing of the Juan de Fuca Strait as a training swim. She struck out from Victoria and headed for Port Angeles. The tidal currents, however, pushed the young swimmer off course, forcing her to aim for a point 5 miles east of her goal.

The bone-chilling waters eventually took their toll, and Marilyn lost consciousness 5½ miles from the finish. Cliff Lumsden and the other crew members dove in to rescue Marilyn and rushed her to a hospital. Cliff stayed with Marilyn throughout her recovery, and then just one week after her failure, he became the second swimmer in history to cross the strait. His time was 11 hours 35 minutes.

While Marilyn was preparing for her second attempt, a Long Beach housewife named Amy Hiland became the first woman to conquer the same stretch of sea. Hiland swam the icy 15 miles in 10 hours 51 minutes.

Marilyn was furious when she learned that another woman had beaten her to it. On August 18, fueled with anger, she struck out from Port Angeles at a rapid pace. Only 10 hours 39 minutes later, she strode ashore

On her second try at the Strait of Juan de Fuca, Marilyn Bell was successful and strode ashore to be greeted by a welcoming committee of 25,000 spectators. This turned out to be Marilyn's last professional swim.

having made a new record. However, since Marilyn was now the fourth swimmer to conquer the strait, the public soon lost interest in the swim—and in Marilyn, who now carried 150 pounds on her 5-foot-2-inch frame and appeared fat. The Juan de Fuca Strait crossing was the final professional swim of her career.

31. Hellespont Solo

At the age of 16 Jack Wheeler suddenly announced to his parents one day that he was going to swim the Hellespont, or Dardanelles. This is the channel that separates Turkey in Asia from Turkey in Europe, a strait which connects the Sea of Marmara with the Aegean Sea. Leander of Greek mythology had crossed here. In that story the young man, Leander, swam each night from the ancient city of Abydos on the Asiatic shore to Sestos on the European shore to visit his girl friend, Hero, a priestess of Aphrodite. On one autumn night a sudden wind blew out the light which Hero had lit to guide her lover across the strait. With no beacon to light his way, Leander drowned in the turbulent sea. Horrified, Hero, too, threw herself into the violent Hellespont.

In more modern times, swimming the Hellespont was a feat performed by the English poet, Lord Byron.

Jack told his parents that he had saved $1,700 for the trip from his home in Glendale, California, to Turkey and that he could do it on a weekend so as not to miss school. He had even phoned the world renowned Greta Andersen for technical advice.

Jack's parents were not terribly surprised, for their precocious son had always performed dramatic and unusual feats. At the age of 12, he had already attained the rank of Eagle Scout. At the age of 14, his television-producer father took him and his family to Europe where he became the youngest American climber in history to scale the Matterhorn in Switzerland. That same summer the teenager played boogie-woogie piano at the Folies-Bergères in Paris in addition to attending school for a while in Moscow.

During the next several years Jack made an eleven-city lecture tour during his Christmas vacations to earn money to buy a boat. He then used his purchase to give water-skiing and skin-diving lessons and to operate a small salvage business. By the time he had completed his junior year in high school, the brilliant, ambitious teenager had won a 4-year scholarship to U.C.L.A.

That summer he used his earnings for a plane ticket to Peru where he set out on a solo mountain-climbing expedition in the Andes. Afterwards Jack hiked through the jungles of Ecuador before returning home. One day while walking near the Amazon River, Jack ran into a family of head-hunting Jivaro Indians. Upon their invitation, he joined them as a house guest for three weeks. At the end of his visit, he accepted a shrunken head as a token of their affection and departed for California in time for school.

That year Jack simultaneously enrolled as a freshman at U.C.L.A. and a high school senior at Hollywood Professional School where he became class president. That fall he decided to attempt the Hellespont swim as a test of his ability. On Friday, November 4, 1960, Jack felt he was ready to leave for Turkey in spite of a severe strep throat and cold which he had acquired during his one training swim in the Pacific. At 5:30 a.m. he left for class at U.C.L.A. although weak from 7 days in bed. After attending an 8 a.m. psychology class, he rushed to the airport to catch a 10:15 flight.

Jack had prepared for his first major solo swim by carrying a kit containing swim fins, trunks, a robe, a towel, a 2-pound jar of Vaseline petroleum jelly, a spare pair of contact lenses, vitamins, cough syrup, and cold medicine. Late that afternoon, however, after he arrived at the airport in Istanbul, he went to claim his well-stocked bag. It was nowhere in sight. After a 20-minute fruitless search, Jack rushed to board a chartered DC-3 for his flight across the Sea of Marmara to Bandirma.

As soon as he arrived, the determined youngster set out to replenish his supplies. In the dark he knocked on shop doors until he managed to find some Vaseline, towels, and swim trunks. Jack quickly hired a taxi to take him to Canakkle, Turkey, 4 hours away and where he was to begin his swim. He arrived late Saturday night and chartered a boat to take him to the starting point. The crew members were five of the best Turkish swimmers available, each of whom had conquered the Hellespont. None had attempted the swim at night, however, or this late in the year. The interpreter advised Jack that the water was only 59°F. (15°C.). The young swimmer donned his new swim trunks and was horrified to see that they hung to his knees. Kicking them off, he decided to swim naked instead.

After coating his body with Vaseline mixed with engine grease, Jack dove into the chilly sea at 12:15 a.m. Surprisingly he decided to swim the entire route with his contact lenses in place. Using a steady crawl stroke, he averaged 1 mile every 24 minutes. Soon, his face and sinuses became racked with pain from the intense cold. Jack turned over on his back to rest, causing himself to drift much too far downstream. His crew yelled warnings to him, but his ears were so numb that he did not hear

them. After only 45 minutes in the icy sea, Jack was completely deaf.

He tried to stay on course by following the lanterns on the boat and by aiming for the moonlit cliffs of Sestos on the European shore. Suddenly at 1 a.m. Jack screamed and sank beneath the chop. When he surfaced 20 feet from the boat, the captain threw him a life preserver. As the boat approached to rescue him, Jack screamed, "No!" and pulled away. He grabbed his right leg, paralyzed with pain, and was appalled to find a swollen, rocklike calf. Treading water, the boy remembered what Greta Andersen had advised him to do in such a situation. He kneaded and squeezed the frozen calf up toward his heart. He refused to panic, and eventually the pain subsided.

Unable to bend his leg any longer, Jack started to swim using a modified breast-stroke while dragging the useless limb. To add to his problems the water teemed with heavy sea traffic near the European shore. One Russian cargo vessel threw a rope over his limp body to tow him clear of the suction produced by the propellers.

At this point Jack was swept under by a violent wave and powerful currents. When he surfaced, he could see his boat way up the channel while he was being helplessly carried out toward the Aegean Sea. He stroked desperately onward for 30 or 40 minutes more but later could not recall the end of the swim. His chilled muscles simply could not respond, and progress was painfully slow.

Only 200 feet from the dangerous rocky shoreline, the captain of his escort boat mercifully fished his body from the Hellespont. The teenager appeared blue, babbled incoherently, and twitched convulsively for hours after being hauled from the sea. At about 3 a.m. Jack regained his senses in a warm Turkish bath, surrounded by admiring Turks pouring steaming water over him. The captain lauded him for his great display of nerve and wished him "Yashaa," or long life.

The California youth slept for 3 hours and

Young Jack Wheeler's prayers of thanks for a successful crossing of the Hellespont were offered up here in the Blue Mosque in Istanbul (on the right). Although his weekend sojourn from California to Turkey was fraught with minor disasters, the 16-year-old adventurer was determined to thank Allah for his good fortune, and even considered becoming a Moslem.

then at dawn boarded his chartered plane which transported him to the Istanbul airport. Since his flight home was not for several hours yet, Jack hired a taxi to take him to the famous Blue Mosque in Istanbul where he gave thanks for his "successful" venture.

While flying home, he attempted to study for an upcoming test but realized that he had been wearing his contact lenses for 70 hours. During his brief stopover in Frankfurt, he recovered his lost bag and finally arrived in Los Angeles at 11:45 Sunday night. The only part of the venture that surprised his parents was that he had driven all the way into Istanbul to visit the Mosque. Jack merely explained that he was considering becoming a Moslem and did not want to miss the opportunity to thank Allah while in the neighborhood!

Dogged Jason Zirganos of Greece never won a marathon so turned to solo swims, a fateful decision.

32. Jason Zirganos' Last Swim

Jason Zirganos was not a fast, flashy swimmer but he took great pride in his ability to endure cold water. The well-padded Greek army major always swam well in marathons, but never won.

He competed every year in the English Channel races, but never did better than fourth place. Eventually he decided to make solo swims in order to boost his sagging ego.

Jason met his match when he attempted to cross the turbulent Bosporus at Istanbul. He lapsed into unconsciousness after battling the icy-cold waters for 4 hours.

In 1953, he attempted a solo crossing of the length of the Bosporus, the channel at Istanbul, Turkey, that connects the Sea of Marmara with the Black Sea. This 15-mile endeavor was unusually tough, because it was autumn and the water was a bone-chilling 46.4°F. (8°C.). Zirganos was hauled from the water in a semi-conscious state after swimming only 4 hours. He did not regain full consciousness until 3 hours after the ordeal.

In 1958, Jason attempted the 26-mile swim around Manhattan Island. Again he waited until autumn when the water temperatures were down into the mid-50's F. (low teens C.). On October 5, Zirganos struck out from the Battery and headed up the East River. Treading water in the Hudson River 23 hours later, Jason appeared blue and incoherent. His crew members again pulled him from the freezing cold river and rushed him to a hospital. This time he required two full days to regain his senses.

Jason was stubborn and determined, however, and the next year at age 45 he stood on the shores of the North Channel of the Irish Sea. This stretch of water had outwitted more swimmers than any other. Both of the top female swimmers, Florence Chadwick and Greta Andersen, had failed on two ill-fated attempts each. Two men did successfully complete the trip. The 252-pound, 33-year-old Tom Blower swam the North Channel in 1947, and Kevin Murphy did it in 1970.

On September 27, 1959, Jason Zirganos added his name to those who had attempted the most demanding swim in the world. At the age of 46 he began the 22-mile swim in water normally ranging from 49° to 53°F. (9.4° to 11.6°C.). After $16\frac{1}{2}$ hours his crew members heard a horrifying gasp and saw their swimmer sink into unconsciousness. The ghostly-looking figure was quickly hauled on board and examined by a doctor. Cutting Zirganos' chest open, the physician found an erratic heartbeat. He began open-heart massage but to no avail. Within 5 minutes the daring Greek was dead. Jason Zirganos had been only 3 miles from his goal when he was defeated by the merciless North Channel waters.

33. Farallon Islands to Golden Gate Bridge

Approximately 30 miles west of San Francisco in the Pacific Ocean lies a group of islands known as the Farallons. The largest of these, Southeast Farallon, with a maximum length of 500 yards, is home for a lone lighthouse tender and a few stray birds. This island has been the launching point for many aspirants trying to swim to the San Francisco or northern mainland.

From this island to Golden Gate Bridge is 30½ miles and, ideally, swimmers would aim for the bridge or Fisherman's Wharf inside the bay in order to be greeted by an audience. The swim from the island to the mainland would be only 21 miles if Bolinas Point were chosen as the finish, but the only greeting an exhausted swimmer would receive there would be from seals and sea gulls.

In the 1960's many swimmers vied for the fame and fortune awaiting the first person to complete this feat. By 1964, 15 of the world's best had tried and failed. Not only did the swimmers have to contend with the 30½-mile course, they had to face water temperatures in the mid-50's to low 60's F. (12° to 16°C.), heavy steamer traffic, powerful, treacherous currents, and even sharks. In 1963 in particular, there were numerous shark attacks on scuba divers near the Farallons. One diver was struck twice by a white shark while spearfishing. He was hospitalized for 4 months and required 500 stitches.

The deadly currents were even more im-portant since a tremendous amount of water gushes daily through the narrow, mile-wide opening into San Francisco Bay. Directly beneath Golden Gate Bridge which spans this entrance, the velocity of the currents flowing out into the ocean can reach 10 miles per hour. If the swim is timed correctly, the athlete can ride the 6-mile-per-hour floodtide toward the bridge. If he hits the ebb tide, however, he is defeated immediately for no one can swim against a 4- to 10-mile-per-hour current.

The swimmer must also avoid the 2,000-foot-wide shipping channel, marked by buoys. Of all of these obstacles, the frigid water temperature is the greatest hazard.

In 1966, the 38-year-old Chicago chemist, Ted Erikson, contemplated attempting the formidable swim. He flew to San Francisco and went directly to the Dolphin Club to find out who had already tried and failed. Greta Andersen was among the names, as was Leonore Modell, one of the youngest swimmers (13) to cross the English Channel. She had been hauled from the water only 3 miles from Golden Gate Bridge.

The Dolphin Club was famous for its annual San Francisco Bay swim which was a popular event in spite of the extreme hazards. One year a tugboat cut directly through a pack of swimmers and severely injured two of them. One lost a hand and the other a foot, but the boat did not even stop. Club members also swam to Alcatraz Island frequently in spite of

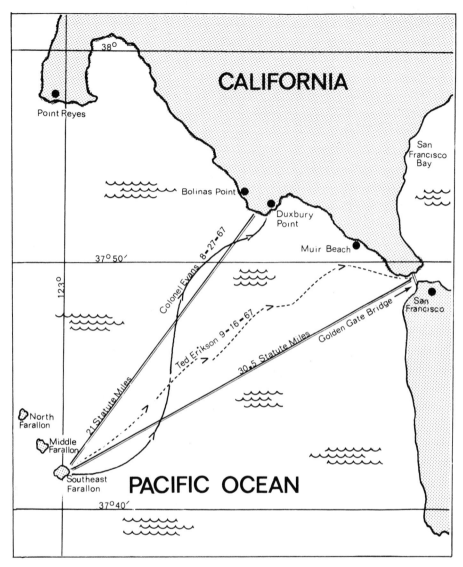

Farallon Islands swims.

claims that no one could survive such an endeavor in the other direction. What non-swimmers did not realize was that at slack tide, a person could almost float ashore either way. In fact, a magician once did exactly that with his hands tied behind his back.

In 1966, the Dolphin Club was disturbed that no one had completed the Farallon Island

swim, so they offered to pay for the escort boat when Ted Erikson said he was interested. He promised that he would devote the entire month of August to an attempt.

On August 15, 1966, Ted was ready, greased, and goggled. At 7:40 a.m. he strode into the 52°F. (11°C.) surf off the Southeast Island. By noon he had covered 8 miles, and the water

On August 15, 1966 Ted Erikson was churning his way through the shark-infested waters between the Farallon Islands and San Francisco, a swim that had bested the top swimmers in the world, which soon included Ted. Although he failed on his first two tries, the following year he became the first swimmer in history to make it.

temperature had risen to 55°F. (12.8°C.). By mid-afternoon the temperatures dropped again, and the first sharks appeared. The captain chased them off with his rifle, but they returned several hours later.

At 8:30 p.m. Ted was only 4 miles from the bridge but was entering the area where the currents became a potential danger. The intense cold slowed his pace to less than 1 mile per hour, but by midnight Ted was within 2 miles of the bridge. The merciless ebb tide, however, was to start flowing in only an hour. For 40 minutes Ted spasmodically flailed at the surf but verged on unconsciousness. Suddenly, he blacked out completely. The crew dove in immediately, tied ropes around the

husky swimmer, and hauled his limp body aboard.

After piling blankets on him, they raced him to the yacht club, but were frantic upon discovering the ambulance was not yet there. Ted's life seemed to be slipping away before their eyes, but they were helpless. Finally sirens filled the night as the ambulance arrived and quickly rushed Ted to a nearby hospital. Since his body temperature was only 90°F. (32.2°C.), doctors placed him in a tub of hot water. His temperature rose to 93°F. (34°C.) in 2 hours, and by the next morning he miraculously was able to leave the hospital. Ted Erickson had spent 17 exhausting hours in the cold water, and yet was already planning a second attempt.

On September 1, 1966, he entered the sea again, but after 10 hours was too nauseated to continue. Apparently the first swim had taken its toll on his endurance.

During the following month, a 40-year-old Hawaiian grandfather, Ike Papke, attempted to swim from the Farallons to Stinson Beach, 10 miles north of the Golden Gate Bridge. The water temperature was still in the mid-50's F. (low teens C.), but this swim was only 22 miles long. With only 1 mile to go, however, the 240-pound swimmer had to be pulled from the sea just as Ted had been.

During that winter Erikson pored over navigation and water temperature charts, and in April began training for the swim in Lake Michigan. Temperatures in the lake were even lower than around the Golden Gate.

At the same time a 41-year-old Army Signal Corps officer, Colonel Stewart A. Evans, was also studying charts and training in the Pacific Ocean. Evans realized that if Ted was unable to swim to the Golden Gate Bridge, he could not either. Therefore, he planned to land at Bolinas Point. While Ted waited for September and warmer water temperatures, Evans planned to try in August.

At 10:15 p.m. on August 27, 1967, the Colonel waded into 58°F. (14.4°C.) seas off the Farallons and headed for Bolinas Point. He did not want still to be in the water when darkness fell the following day, so he maintained a good pace. His boat kept a constant heading even though the tidal currents pulled him north and south of a straight-line distance. For most of the swim Evans had only lemon Jello and carbonated drinks. By 9 a.m. he suffered severe muscle pains in his left shoulder.

At the same time sharks appeared. The crew fired shots at the menacing gray shapes and tried to run them down with the boat, but they circled for over an hour. By 10 a.m. Evans, unable to lift his pain-racked arm, realized that if he did not land at Duxbury Point, he would be faced with an extra mile swim to the mainland. Evans picked up his pace slightly

and was encouraged by the Dolphin Club members who swam next to him in relays.

Only 400 yards from shore, the shoulder pain overpowered him once again, forcing him to stop to let it subside. Finally, with a crowd of 500 admirers cheering the exhausted figure on, he reached the surf line and started wading in. Barely 10 feet from shore he fell, however, and the crowd yelled, "Crawl!"

At 12:03 p.m. after 13 hours 46 minutes in the chilling ocean, Evans crawled ashore and kissed his jubilant wife. Colonel Evans had become the first person in history to swim from the Farallon Islands to the mainland, a distance in this case of 21 miles.

Ted Erikson had only one choice now if he was to set a record. He had to put his 6 months of training and over 800 miles of swimming to use to reach the Golden Gate Bridge. This was to be the final marathon swim of his career.

The day of his swim was unusually windless with the ocean looking like a lake. At dawn, Ted covered himself with grease and shark repellent and entered the 60°F. (15.6°C.) seas at 7:22 a.m. With direct broadcasts being made throughout the day to a local radio station, KSFO, the historic swim received much publicity. Within an hour a heavy fog set in, but the water temperature rose slightly. Pacers took turns swimming with Ted and by 11:10 a.m., he had covered 7 miles. Soon afterward he accepted his first feeding of peaches and dextrose.

Ted remained in high spirits and was amused to see four sea lions frolicking alongside him. By mid-afternoon Point Reyes was visible to his left, but the bridge in front of him was shrouded in fog. Plagued by his usual fear of being left behind in the ocean, Ted demanded that the escort boat stay by his side. Scores of ships and fishing vessels came within sight of the swimmer as he drew within 8 miles of the bridge. The tides continually carried Erikson to the north until at 9:14 p.m. he was only a half mile off Point Bonita.

At this time Colonel Evans, who had been

Colonel Stewart Evans, while trying to shake water out of his ear, is plied with questions about how it feels to be the first person to make a successful swim between the Farallons and the mainland. Evans came ashore at rugged Point Bolinas.

with him, dove into the cold sea and paced Ted for a while. Soon a sightseeing boat with glaring television lights pulled under the bridge, and a pilot boat shot up a flare. At 10 p.m. Ted swam directly beneath the bridge, becoming the first athlete in history to swim from the Farallons to San Francisco. Two of the pacers pulled Erikson onto a raft where he appeared to be in good condition. Smiling and coherent, Ted posed for pictures briefly, then got into the escort boat, and headed for Aquatic Park. The Dolphin Pier was bursting with spectators, television cameras, and newspapermen when the blanket-clad figure disembarked onto the dock. He soon was whisked away to a hot shower and a sauna and felt so good that he even went to nearby Fisherman's Wharf for dinner and beer.

After chatting with the press and jokingly telling them he was 62 years old, he contentedly left for home at 12:30 a.m.

34. Florida Keys to Freeport, Bahamas

It was billed as the "Swim of the Century" but eventually became the "Drift of the Century" instead. Ingenious Benson Huggard vowed that he would swim from the Florida Keys to Freeport in the Bahamas, an unprecedented distance of 165 miles!

The 35-year-old New York plainclothes policeman was determined finally to make some money from his distance swimming abilities. Since he was amiable and handsome, he hoped to gain endorsements and invitations to talk-shows after his successful swim. He had never won a professional race, but what he lacked in speed, he made up for in determination. In 1971, Huggard became only the seventh American to swim from England to France, but he did it in a relatively slow 15 hours. In 1974, he was a member of a relay team which swam from France to England and back again.

Huggard struck on the idea of swimming from Florida to the Bahamas while attending a dinner for Jacques Cousteau. The Bahamas Promotion Board immediately became intrigued, and soon sponsors came forth with money.

Since sharks were the greatest hazard in this swim, Huggard and a friend, Dick Boullianne, spent $5,800 building a cage to take along. It was made of 9-gauge aluminum cyclone fencing and could withstand the impact of 4,000 pounds per square inch. The cage was 20 feet long by 10 feet wide by $6\frac{1}{2}$ feet deep, had an open top, and was floated on two Styrofoam pontoons.

Although kick-boards are illegal in races, Huggard, who had held the "open swimming record" at one time, tied his legs together and held a board between his ankles for buoyancy. He also used a normally illegal swimming aid—swim fins—for 91 miles.

Huggard began his historic swim in May, 1975, by ordering his crew not to pull him from the water unless he was dead. He started the journey outside the shark cage, but within 6 minutes of the start, he spotted three shark fins circling around him. He immediately jumped into the cage being towed by his escort boat.

Huggard swam well until 2:35 p.m. when he stopped for his first hourly feeding. At that point he was joined in his cage by two yellow-tail jacks. Since one was about 18 inches long and the other closer to 12 inches, he named them Mutt and Jeff. The two fish kept Huggard company for 4 hours until suddenly Mutt devoured Jeff and departed.

Huggard's first severe trouble arose about midnight when the wind gathered force and huge swells rocked the escort boat. As the tiny ship bobbed like a cork in the vast ocean, the crew grew extremely seasick. The cage being towed 150 feet behind the boat, however, was in much worse condition. It was literally coming apart at the seams, and the front already sagged 4 feet beneath the surface of the waves.

Huggard, feeling more and more like fish bait, could clearly see the dark 6- or 7-foot long shapes swimming beneath him and nosing at the fragile cage. To make matters worse,

Benson Huggard, 35-year-old policeman from Freeport, New York, shattered the world record for long distance ocean swims when he swam 173 miles. It was dubbed the "Swim of the Century."

chunks of the cage's Styrofoam floats were coming loose. In spite of these problems Huggard and his crew slowly made their way through the Bermuda Triangle that night.

By dawn most of the cage was submerged, and a Portuguese man-of-war had slipped over the top and stung the helpless swimmer on one hand and both feet. By putting the wounded hand in his mouth, he caused his

tongue to swell. Huggard downed a Darvon and Coke to try to alleviate the excruciating pain, but to no avail.

At this point his grandmother, who previously had offered him $10,000 if he would not attempt the swim, now raised her offer to $20,000 to stop. Huggard refused.

By morning the winds had died down enough so that the crew was able to repair the damaged pontoons. From 7:15 to 9 a.m. Huggard sat on the edge of the cage swallowing peaches and Coke as the Gulf Stream gently carried him north. The incredible swim had now become the "Tow of the Century."

That afternoon Huggard became violently ill and banged against the walls of his cage. Watching in agony, the crew had to leave the retching swimmer alone, helpless. Fifteen minutes later he miraculously started swimming again. Their troubles were not over, however, for soon the Styrofoam began splitting apart again. Boullianne desperately tried to fix the pontoons, but suddenly without warning the entire cage sank beneath the surface.

Huggard wanted to continue on anyway, but was overruled by his crew, who dragged the frustrated swimmer on board. A large crowd greeted the weary team as they pulled into the Big Game Fishing Club. Although Huggard had been dragged from the Atlantic short of his goal, he set a new distance record for any swimming Hall of Fame. Averaging more than 5 miles per hour due to the effects of the Gulf Stream, Huggard had covered an astounding 173 miles.

III. THE DISTANCE BICYCLE RACER

Jacques Anquetil

Belgium's Freddy Maertens gleefully wins the finishing sprint of the second lap of the Paris-Nice event, one of the major European bicycling races.

35. Winners on Wheels

His legs are shaved smooth so that bandages can be changed less painfully. His enormous thighs seem out of place on his lean, wiry body, and his veins protrude like those on the legs of a racehorse. Hollow cheeks and darkened eyes seem chiseled into his tense face, and his heart pounds at a mere 40 beats per minute.

With the Alps behind him and the Pyrenees ahead of him, he refuels with chicken, sandwiches, fruit, and a syrup made of two pounds of sugar dissolved in water. He smiles and jokes with the others in his pack, thinking that this particular day of the Tour is an easy one since the route is flat, and he is only pedaling

110 miles. He relieves himself as the wheels of his fragile bike roll on since he will not be dismounting for many hours yet.

As he passes by the hero-worshipping spectators, he wordlessly grabs the food and drink they humbly offer him. He is about 5 feet 7 inches tall, weighs about 140 pounds, is between 27 and 32 years old, and although he is married and has children, young women chase him incessantly.

When he is not racing, he lives lavishly and flamboyantly on his $100,000 annual earnings. He owns a very expensive home, carries exorbitantly high insurance, and in the off-season hunts, fishes, brags, and recuperates from the injuries characteristic of his profession. This year he will crash five or six times, and at least once before ending his racing career he will be involved in a serious accident. Although he will bear scars for the rest of his life, his name will be revered throughout Europe.

This is a profile of the average racer in Europe's most brutal, dramatic, and popular sport—bicycle road racing, which can be the supreme endurance test. In addition to mental and physical strength, the sport demands possibly more courage than any other athletic event. In most European races, an average day's ride covers 150 miles or more and requires pedaling for an exhausting 7 hours non-stop while straddling a hard, narrow bicycle seat. It is not uncommon for racers to collapse during the agonizing ordeal. Those with failing strength continue on unsteadily, pedal to mountain summits, and then descend at speeds of 60 miles per hour or more. Often the mind becomes muddled and the eyes bleary as the racer precariously skids through hairpin turns.

In addition to his vulnerable mental state, his equipment, too, may be a dangerous handicap. At extremely high speeds the lightweight aluminum bikes with their narrow tires can easily go out of control. For these reasons, bloody, and even fatal, accidents are an integral part of bicycle road races. In each major event at least half a dozen athletes suffer broken bones or fractured skulls. Whenever a cyclist falls, the concrete, gravel, or cobblestone road may mercilessly scar him for life. Since 100 or more men may enter a single race, massive collisions can occur, and occasionally an athlete plunges over a cliff or head-on into a tree. The more minor injuries range from chronic saddle sores to side effects of stimulants which are commonly taken.

It may seem surprising that bicycle road racing is a team sport. Each star is surrounded by his retinue of *domestiques*. These are assistants who ride in front of him to serve as a windbreak or to interfere strategically with the other stars, and whenever his bike breaks down, the star simply takes another from one of these teammates. In spite of their racing abilities, the *domestiques* rarely gain either fame or fortune but instead vie for small prizes. The stars do not usually begin their careers as assistants but often become known on the indoor track circuit first. There they race against the clock, set records, and make a name for themselves before going on the road.

Each year the cyclists begin training in February for the road races to be held that season. They cover more than 120 miles each day through the roads and mountains of the Riviera. The first races of the year are held there and generally are won by rookies. The season's first major race runs from Paris to Nice and is the undoing of many cyclists. The punishing pace is approximately 25 miles per hour, a speed which leads to many injuries and early defeats. Those that survive this race across plains and over mountains eventually cover 900 miles in 9 days. To the veteran racers this event is merely a warm-up for the ones to follow. There is the Giro d'Italia (Tour of Italy) which is a 3-week marathon; the Bordeaux-to-Paris, France, race (372.6 miles); the 180-mile Milan-to-San Remo, Italy, event; the Tour of Egypt; the Tour of Tunisia; and the Tour of Spain. Of course, the most famous and popular race is the arduous 3-week Tour de France

The four-man team from Poland of Lujan Ris, Ryszard Skurkowski, Stanislaw Szozda and Mytnik ride to a gold medal in the 100-kilometer time-trial race of the world cycling championships at Granollers, outside Barcelona, Spain, on August 29, 1973.

which covers approximately 2,700 miles. The winner of that epic event becomes an overnight hero in France and throughout Europe.

Canada, known for its distance swimmers, also excels in distance bicycle racing. The Tour du St. Laurent covers 794 miles, while the Quebec-to-Montreal race spans 170 miles. The latter is sponsored by the Canadian newspaper, *La Presse*.

The most famous events which have been held in the United States are the Tour of Somerville, New Jersey; the Eastern Seaboard championships held in Yonkers, New York; the Arthur Longsjo Memorial Race in Fitchburg, Massachusetts; the Grand Prix of Long Island; the Connecticut Valley championships in

Hartford, Connecticut; and the Chicago-to-Elgin, Illinois, race.

The organization which presides over this sport on a world-wide basis is the Union Cycliste International (UCI), which was founded in 1900. It represents 71 nations, and regulates both amateur and professional competition. The National Cycling Association (NCA) is the United States representative to UCI and deals with professional racers in the United States, while the Amateur Bicycle League of America governs the amateurs.

The bicycle first gained great popularity in the 1800's, and the first distance racing record was established in 1883. In that year, H. L. Cortis pedaled for 24 hours, covering 200 miles

Parading through downtown Milan, Italy, prior to the 180-mile race between Milan and San Remo in 1975 are 199 cyclists from seven nations. They are shown here stopping traffic in front of the Filarete Tower of Sforzesco Castle.

and 300 yards with a speed of 9 miles per hour. In the following decade cycling became the favorite outdoor recreation for Americans, Canadians, and Britons. In 1891, Madison Square Garden launched the beginning of the 6-day indoor races, and a record for that event was established 7 years later when Charlie Miller rode for 142 hours covering 2,093.4 miles. Even these early endurance races took their toll since many athletes were hospitalized from exhaustion. International cycling competition began in 1893, but the American athletes declined in calibre after a fire destroyed the New York Velodrome in 1929.

An unofficial record for the maximum speed attained over one mile was set in 1962 by a Frenchman named Jose Meiffret. He allegedly reached the astounding speed of 127.16 miles per hour, riding behind a windshield attached to a motorcycle. An even higher speed was attained behind a windshield mounted on a car on Bonneville Salt Flats, Utah. The bicyclist, Dr. Allan V. Abbott of San Bernardino, California, reached 140.5 m.p.h. and averaged 138.7 over a mile.

International cycling competition produces winners in fourteen categories including three for women. Both road and track racing are represented in the Olympic Games which crown seven champions. The most highly esteemed competition, however, is the Tour de France which was originated in 1903 by a journalist named Henri Desgrange.

Jose Meiffret of France claimed to have reached a speed of 127.16 miles per hour while riding behind this large windshield mounted on a motorcycle which preceded him.

36. The Tour de France: The World Series of Cycling

Winning the Tour de France is cycling's highest honor—greater than that of capturing the world championship. Although it has been compared to baseball's World Series, no other country has any sport which really equals the emotional impact of the Tour. Even though 15 million spectators line the roads during the race and millions more watch on television, no one actually sees much of the incredible event, and yet, this does not appear to matter. The Tour is really much more than a bicycle race. It is a social, patriotic, and semi-religious tragicomedy, marked with passion, conflict, humor, violence, and sometimes even death.

In every non-war year since its inception in 1903, some 100 or more dust- and blood-caked cyclists have pedaled through 800 or so communities, from historic European cities to tiny, rural villages. They have crossed over vast plains; pedaled up winding, twisting roads to mountain peaks over 7,000 feet high; breezed over the borders of France, Belgium, Spain, Switzerland, and Italy without ever showing a single passport.

These riders battle it out for 25 or 30 days, reaching speeds of up to 60 miles per hour, suffering flesh-tearing falls, and covering almost 3,000 miles—with all of Europe watching and waiting. Each day is a separate stage in the race, and each one has its own winner and its own story. About half of the entrants finish this race, considered to be the most punishing endurance event in the world, and all of them are considered international heroes. The French newspapers refer passionately and reverently to these men as "demigods, Apollos, eagles," and so on, for they have survived broken bones, flesh wounds, sunstroke, exhaustion, frostbite, saddle sores, lost toenails, and drugs. The winner of the entire event is not only a god in the eyes of all Europe, but he becomes a millionaire overnight.

Those witnessing the race for the first time are amazed at the fast pace set from the beginning. The lean, anxious cyclists pedal slowly toward the starting line, and sprint at full speed as they begin the first leg of the long race. They average 20 to 25 miles per hour throughout the race in spite of numerous flat tires, impasses where the bikes must be carried, and steep, treacherous mountain grades. In flat stretches the cyclists maintain about 35 miles per hour and on downhill runs may reach 60 m.p.h.

The *domestiques* take their places, pacing the one or two members of their 10-man team who have a chance of winning. They serve as a windbreak, keep a close watch on the other stars, and harass their opponents openly. If a rival breaks away, they chase him even if they must sacrifice themselves for the rest of the day. The winning team collects $100,000 offered by the sponsors, two French newspapers, *L'Equipe* and *Le Parisien Libéré*. The *domestiques* divide

On the 10th lap of the 1968 Tour de France, the pack glides through a cool glade in the Landes Forest between Bordeaux and Bayonne, a welcome respite in the grueling 3,000-mile ordeal.

the prize among themselves while the star makes his income from endorsements.

As the spectators line the roads awaiting a glimpse of their heroes, they fill the endless hours with gossip, card playing, and picnics, until finally spotting the first publicity vans in the distance. The French, being avid lovers of lampoon, wait in anticipation and amusement for what is to follow—a comic relief in the form of a gaudy, colorful, commercialized caravan 30 miles long, with trucks blaring music and advertising slogans through loudspeakers; cars in the shape of products such as lemons and beer bottles; sponsors tossing free samples of gum, toys, and so on, into the crowd—all this to the tune of the sirens and horns of a police escort. Behind this cavalcade are the officials and newspapermen, followed by the flag car.

The motley procession passes by a given point for a full 90 minutes before the racers come into view, rumps in the air and legs pumping like pistons. With the whirring of wheels and the clicking of pedals, they flash by at speeds of up to 60 miles per hour, wearing advertising as the cars do in the Indianapolis 500. Close on their tails are the mechanics who navigate cars laden with spare parts and topped off with spare wheels on the roofs. The caravan may be made up of as many as 350 automobiles, trucks, and motorcycles and yet, it, like the cyclists, passes over borders without presenting even one passport. The border guards merely cheer them on.

During the procession one year, a Tour car careened out of control into a crowd of spectators, near Valenciennes, France, and injured twelve fans. The race officials, apparently unperturbed, merely left their names with the

French champion Jacques Anquetil is cheered on by a group of young fans at Besançon, France, during the 1963 Tour de France. Spectators such as these will wait for days until their hero passes by.

local police and continued on their way. It went without saying that none of the usual barriers, customs, or formalities prevail during the 3,000-mile, month-long race.

Passion dominates the annual event as the onlookers use all tactics imaginable to assist their heroes or stop their foes. As a star comes within range, his fans may greet him with a welcome spray of cool water from a garden hose, a drink, or even a discreet push as he struggles up a steep hill. A star's enemies often throw tacks on the road, taunt him with withheld canteens of water, or in extreme cases pull him off his bike and attack him viciously.

Violence has plagued the Tour since its inception. In the first year of the event an Italian won the race, but the following year he was harassed by supporters of a French racer. A mob near St. Etienne attacked the helpless cyclist and injured one of his teammates. From Nîmes to Toulouse, the assaults grew more violent forcing local police to use their guns to protect the racers. As a further precaution, officials tried pre-dawn starts and rerouting the race, but on the last day's ride to Paris the cyclists were blocked by fallen trees and stacks of hay. When they stopped to survey the prob-lem, local Frenchmen swarmed in on the unsuspecting athletes.

The Tour de France is continually beset by problems. In 1966, an army of 12,000 police-men patrolled the route. Vandals threw tacks on the road that year, forcing the racers to carry six or seven spare tires around their necks, prepared for the worst. In 1913, tacks had eliminated 24 cyclists from the race in one day.

In another incident a rider named Duboc took a drink offered by an onlooker and was poisoned. One year, the Belgian team quit the event entirely to protest the spectators' throw-ing of objects at them. Often riders have to disguise themselves to pass through an enemy village safely. The unsuccessful ones find their bikes have been sabotaged while they slept.

Not all the injuries are inflicted by the enemy, however, for the famous cyclist, Péllisier, was badly hurt by an overwhelming mob of admirers as he crossed the finish line one year in Paris. In a more serious tragedy, René Pottier, who had just won the 1906 Tour, was found dead soon afterward, apparently a suicide victim. His brother, André, competed in the Tour two years later, but when he reached the summit of Ballon d'Alsace, he

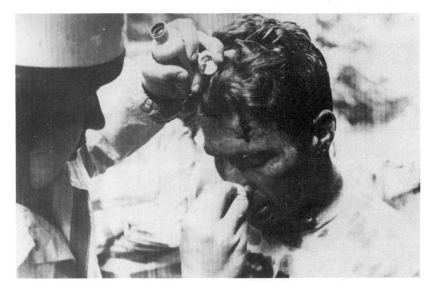

Doctors are always on call during major bicycle races. Accidents are frequent, some minor, some serious, some fatal. Here, Raymond Poulidor submits to the ministrations of a Tour de France doctor after a bad fall in the Pyrenees during the 1973 Tour.

"The Eagle of Toledo," Frederico Bahamontes, crosses the finish line to win the eighth stage of the 1964 Tour de France in 1964. One year, after the great Spanish cyclist lost popularity with his fans, he was jeeringly labeled, "The Turtle from Toledo."

stopped at the monument erected in memory of his brother. André broke down and sobbed, meanwhile losing valuable time in the race. He eventually finished 17th. In another year's Tour, a Spaniard named Cepeda fell from his bike, but managed to struggle back on and continue the race. He collapsed soon after the finish and died in a hospital of a fractured skull.

In the 1958 Tour, André Darrigade entered Paris in the lead during the sixth stage of the event. As he blazed over the finish line, an official unintentionally stepped into his path. After untangling the web of bloody, broken bones and mangled spokes, Darrigade in bandages managed to complete the lap of honor. The official, however, was not so fortunate. He died not long after.

However, in spite of accidents and un-warranted violence, the Tour de France lives on.

Often when tragedy strikes a cyclist, it is in a more subtle form than death. The psychological pressures of defeat and victory are extremely destructive. One year the Spaniard, Brambella, lost the race on the final day of the Tour and afterwards sank into a deep depression. He was later found burying his bike in a grave he had dug behind his house.

The victors, too, reach a mentally precarious position, for they can never live up to the god-like image the public holds of them. The Spanish racer, Frederico Bahamontes, fell victim to just such a fate. Upon winning the Tour de France one year, the Spaniard was named the "Eagle of Toledo," and when he returned home, he was idolized by all. A parade

149

and reception were held in his honor, the mayor of Toledo granted him land on which to build a house, and the cardinal sent his blessing. Again, revering him as if a god, a sculptor created a statue of the great athlete's legs.

Bahamontes returned to France for a while to fulfil obligations and make more money from the race. When he finally went home to Spain, he again had to prove himself, this time by fighting and killing a bull. For the rest of the year the Spaniard was honored by all of Europe. Of course, he was expected to compete again in the Tour de France the following year, but he unexpectedly dropped out on the second day. Although he claimed that he was sick, the demanding fans who had idolized him the previous year, now called him a bum. They mockingly named him the "Turtle from Toledo."

Bahamontes' fans were harsh on their former hero, for during the previous spring he had crashed while descending a mountain and had broken his leg. When he entered the Tour of Spain several months later, he had raced poorly and was booed loudly. Unable to accept this turn of events, Bahamontes grabbed a tire pump and viciously beat a jeering spectator with it. Disqualified for his inexcusable conduct, he returned home in disgrace.

The race is not always so tragic but often is almost like a slapstick comedy routine. One year an African racer named Zaaf broke away from his pack and took the lead. He began quenching his thirst with wine, and soon became so wobbly and unsteady that he fell from his bike. Shaken from his drunken stupor, he immediately leaped back on but headed in the wrong direction! He had no inkling of what he had done until suddenly, horrified, he spotted his competitors heading straight for him.

All sorts of racing tactics have been tried in the Tour, some humorous, some deceitful, and some vicious. The Spaniard, Bahamontes, also was known for blazing up the mountainous stages of the event and then dismounting at the summit. While waiting for his competitors to come into view he rested, ate ice cream, and joked with the spectators. Then as the others approached, Bahamontes leaped on his bike and rode away. Although these demoralizing tactics gained him a victory only once, the Spaniard collected many prizes for being the first over a mountain.

Henri Alavoine employed the unusual gimmick of grabbing onto the door handle of an official's car as it passed by and then engaging in an argument over a certain rule. Since the car kept on moving, he obtained a free ride.

In 1935, a Belgian named Romain Maes gained a small lead on the first day of the Tour. He managed to reach a railroad crossing just before a long freight train approached. Of course, the other cyclists were trapped behind it, allowing Maes to stretch his lead to an incontestable distance. He held onto that lead for the rest of the Tour.

In most Tours it is said that the race can be won or lost in the mountains, which sometimes reach a height of 7,000 feet or more. Often the mountain roads are closed to automobile traffic as the Tour approaches so spectators must arrive early in the morning. Excitement grows to a frenzied pitch throughout the day, and as the lead bike comes into view, a raucous cheer is heard. This is one point where an onlooker can get more than a glimpse of his hero, since the athletes pedal very slowly while approaching the summit.

The cyclists often must climb 16 or more miles on a 17° gradient and usually must fight blustery mountain winds as well. Exhausted, they pedal past the spectators at a snail's pace. Police hold back the crowds, but usually someone breaks through and splashes water on his idol to revive him. Others hand the cyclists newspapers which they tuck under their jerseys to serve as windbreaks on the ride down. Speeds of up to 60 miles an hour are reached on the trip back, and it may be 15 or more miles before the bicyclists pedal again.

The high speeds and the hairpin turns demand enormous courage and skill of the

The strain is showing as Gastone Nencini of Italy and Marcel Janssens of Belgium (leading) are the first to get to the top of Galibier Pass in the French Alps during the 10th lap of the Tour de France in 1957.

cyclist. At the bottom the men are cold and stiff but soon must climb again. The mountains can make or break a rider, and usually there are no spectators below the summit to cheer him on. Both the climb and the descent are notoriously debilitating and dangerous, and every year these steep grades take their toll.

The Italian, Gastone Nencini, is exceptionally daring on mountain descents. In the 1960 Tour, he and Roger Rivière of France raced

neck-and-neck 15 minutes ahead of the pack. Descending the treacherous roads in the Pyrenees, Nencini hurtled his bike down the steep grade, sliding through turns and rarely braking at all. Rivière followed close behind and copied every move. Eventually, Nencini skidded around a sharp turn which Rivière was unable to complete. He exploded through a retaining wall and plunged 65 feet down the mountain. As he lay among the boulders unable

France's Roger Rivière, shown here speeding round the wooden track of the Vigorelli Velodrome in Milan in 1957, only three years later met with disaster when he plummeted down a mountainside during the Tour de France and was paralyzed.

to move, his spine snapped in two locations, he believed no one had seen him go over the cliff.

Fortunately, a teammate, Louis Rostallon, did see Rivière and summoned a helicopter which rescued him from the deep ravine. Rivière survived but was partially paralyzed. At the time of his accident he was 25, earning $100,000 a year, and held the world record for number of miles pedaled in an hour.

Nencini won the Tour that year, but the next year he, too, went out of control, careering down a mountain. He hurtled over a wall and landed in a deep gorge. In spite of suffering a head injury and broken back, he lived to race again. He lost something in the fall, however, for he never won another race after that.

The closest finish in the history of the Tour de France occurred in 1964. Jacques Anquetil, the Babe Ruth of cycling, was trying to top off his four previous, consecutive victories in the Tour with an astounding fifth win. The dashing, blond millionaire, however, was closely pursued throughout the race by France's beloved Raymond Poulidor, a sort of Jimmy Stewart type. Amiable, shy, and poor, he never quite captures first place, but is often the favorite of the spectators. Although an excellent racer in the mountains, he lacks Anquetil's shrewd racing tactics and brilliant use of the *domestiques*. In the exciting 1964 Tour, Poulidor, true to form, finished the arduous, lengthy event only 55 seconds behind unbeatable Anquetil.

In 1966, the French newspapers predicted a

The victors of the closest finish in the history of the Tour de France—Jacques Anquetil on the left, first place, and Raymond Poulidor, who came in a scant 55 seconds later in the 1964 race. Here they make their tour of honor at the Parc des Princes Stadium in Paris.

renewed battle between these two great cyclists. This time Anquetil and Poulidor decided to work as a team at first. They were to act as windbreaks for each other until they gained a solid lead over their competitors. Once they had pulled in front, they would battle each other for the ultimate victory. Trouble brewed early in the race, however, and their plans quickly deteriorated into an all-out war. Poulidor was impeded near the start by an official car, and Anquetil left him behind.

Later, while they childishly fought each other, a German named Rudy Altig took possession of the *maillot jaune* or yellow shirt and wore it for almost half of the race. This is worn by the leader of a particular lap to signify that he is in front. As they passed through the coal and steel country in northern and western France, an Italian took the lead, and eventually during the 11th lap a French *domestique*, Jean-Claude Lebaube, wore the jersey. Anquetil and Poulidor remained about 7 minutes behind the leader.

Poulidor and Anquetil finally ended their personal feud and gradually gained on the leader. They were unable, however, to get closer than 5 minutes from 25-year-old Lucien Aimar, the new possessor of the *maillot jaune*. Aimar was a *domestique* on Anquetil's team and was only in his second year of professional competition. At the end of 17 stages of the 22-stage race, Anquetil surprisingly offered to

The pack advances through heavy rain during the 1966 Tour. In the lead are Ugo Colombo of Italy, Giuseppe Fezzardi of Italy, Raymond Poulidor of France and Raymond DeLisle of France.

154

France's Lucien Aimar dons the "maillot jaune," or yellow shirt, after becoming over-all leader in a lap in the 1966 Tour. He went on to finish in first place.

act as a *domestique* for Aimar. All of France approved of this gallant gesture.

Poulidor was furious at Anquetil's treachery and cleverly broke away, recapturing 49 seconds from Aimar's lead. Strangely enough, Anquetil did not chase after him, but later explained that at the top of Grand St. Bernard Pass, an onlooker had drenched him with ice water. A chronic pulmonary problem was reactivated by this, and he had difficulty breathing.

The following day Anquetil was again soaked, but this time it was by a sudden thunderstorm. He faltered, eventually stopped, and reluctantly announced to his manager, "C'est fini" ("It's all over"). He was rushed to a hospital where they diagnosed a serious chest cold and fever.

Three days later a jubilant crowd of 46,000 at Parc des Princes greeted Aimar as he crossed the finish in first place. A Dutchman, Jan Janssen, followed close on his heels only 67 seconds back. Amiable and persistent Poulidor pedaled over the finish a mere 122 seconds behind Aimar. In the final 32-mile lap from Rambouillet to Paris, Poulidor's sprint had cut the victor's lead in half.

Aimar and Janssen received a frenzied, noisy ovation from the huge crowd of admirers, but when Poulidor accepted his bouquet and kiss, the spectators went wild shouting, "Poulidor! Poulidor!" The exhausted country boy smiled feebly, accepting his destiny as France's most beloved loser.

The Drug Controversy

In 1965, Britain's Tom Simpson became the first of his countrymen to win the world cycling championship. At the age of 29, he found himself in the lead pack of the 1967 Tour de France. He had started from Marseilles and was climbing the winding, narrow road up the 6,273-foot-high Mont Ventoux. Suddenly, as he approached the summit, he began to falter. His head swam and his bike wavered, abruptly hurling him into a cliff. Unconscious, he was airlifted out of the rugged area by helicopter and rushed to a hospital. Unfortunately, it was too late for he had died on the way.

When they emptied his pockets, they discovered two half-empty vials, one bearing the medical trade name for "bennies."

One night during the 1966 Tour while Raymond Poulidor was receiving a rubdown, a doctor and two policemen barged into the room. They demanded a specimen to be analyzed for evidence of drug usage. Sponsors of the race as well as a French Cabinet member realized that amphetamines had always been an integral part of bicycle racing, but they were determined to end their use. Although the athletes had protested that there was no other way to maintain the inhuman pace of the race,

Tom Simpson of Great Britain here has the edge on Rudy Altig of West Germany as they head for the finish of the 167-mile race in the 1965 world professional road race championship at San Sebastian, Spain. Only two years later, he died of a drug overdose during the Tour de France.

in 1966 new laws had been enacted, imposing a $1,000 fine and a year in jail for violators.

During the night, word of the inspection passed quickly and secretly among the other racers. The next day the athletes mounted their bikes and headed for Bayonne at the leisurely pace of 10 miles per hour. Within a few minutes the entire Tour drew to an abrupt halt as each racer dismounted and began walking his bike down the road. The meaning behind the strike was that if any charges were filed against Poulidor, the race would be boycotted. The officials heard the message loud and clear, and since so much money was at stake, they dropped the entire matter.

In 1966, Jacques Anquetil also faced drug charges after the 25-mile Liège-Bastogne-Liège race. At one point during the event Anquetil suddenly sprinted away from the pack and out

of sight. He beat the second place finisher by 4 minutes 53 seconds. Afterwards, the race physician demanded a urine specimen, but Anquetil refused. He insisted that the doctor was too late and that he was above suspicion since he had been a racer for so many years.

The Belgian officials said that it was a law, and he was immediately fined $200 for not complying. The French cyclist vowed that he would not pay a cent and that he would never race in Belgium again. Millionaire Anquetil then hired a famous trial lawyer, René Floriot, to appeal the case. The athlete was finally ordered to pay the fine, but all of Europe mocked the Belgian officials.

After Tom Simpson's death, Jacques Anquetil made the blunt comment, "Cyclists have been taking dope for 50 years. I take dope. So do all the leading bicycle riders . . . Obviously, we could do without dope in a race, but then we would pedal by at 15 miles per hour (instead of the usual 25 m.p.h.). It wouldn't look like much of anything. Since we are constantly asked to go faster and to make an even greater effort, we are obliged to take stimulants. People ask too much of us."

Those pressuring the athletes to push themselves harder are generally the large companies that pay the cyclists for wearing their advertising. Before his death, Simpson earned about $100,000 each year from Peugeot, the French car manufacturer, and B.P., the British Petroleum corporation.

Officials apparently were aware of these problems since they had unsuccessfully tried to remove the commercialism in the Tour by ordering the cyclists to compete on national teams. They also tried to stop the athletes from wearing jerseys bearing advertising front and back. The sponsors, however, fought the ruling vehemently, declaring that the Tour was a major portion of their advertising and that it could not be cut off. The officials relented,

apparently finding no easy solution to the drug problem.

In 1968, strict drug law enforcement was attempted, but it forced many of the world champions (Eddy Merckx of Belgium, Jacques Anquetil of France, and Felice Gimondi and Gianni Motta of Italy) to boycott the Tour. Those favored to win were France's Roger Pingeon, the previous year's victor, and irrepressible Raymond Poulidor.

The "Mineral Water Tour," as it became known, started along the western coast of France with few exciting incidents. Finally, after the halfway point, Pingeon completed several spectacular maneuvers, putting some thrill back into the race. During the 18th stage, however, as he rode from St. Etienne to Grenoble, a cold downpour drenched the cyclists. Pingeon was always affected more than others by poor weather and knew he would have to summon all his strength. Heading for Grenoble, 40 miles away, he courageously sprinted as fast as possible, leaving his competitors behind.

"Cyclists have been taking dope for 50 years. I take dope. So do all the leading bicycle riders . . . People ask too much of us," was Jacques Anquetil's comment after Simpson's death.

157

The others steadily rode on while conserving their energy and keeping an eye on each other. The next two stages were in the rugged mountains, and Pingeon slowly lost much of his lead as he grew weary.

As the athletes began the final day's ride on Sunday, July 21, 1968, no one knew what the outcome would be. The possible victors included Jan Janssen, Ferdinand Bracke, and Van Springel in addition to Pingeon. It was an unprecedented ending since the results of the 3,000-mile, 3-week-long race were to be determined in the final 10 miles to Paris, which were to be essentially individual time trials.

The finish line was the velodrome in the suburb of Vincennes, and it was packed with tens of thousands of anxious fans. A huge Dutch contingent awaited Janssen. As each cyclist entered the arena, their times were displayed on an electronic board.

Janssen was the first to cross the finish, followed closely by Van Springel. Janssen had won by a mere 38 seconds! The crowd roared as the Dutchman was enveloped in tears, laughter, and kisses and carried off on a fan's shoulders. With or without the dangerous amphetamines, the Tour de France is certainly the most brutal, exciting, and emotional contest on earth.

Jubilant Karel Rottiers raises his arms in triumph as he crosses the finish line to win the third lap of the Tour in Versailles in 1975. Belgian superstar Eddy Merckx, shown in the dead center, came in sixth.

37. "Cannibal Eddy" Merckx

Belgium's lean and hungry Eddy Merckx (pronounced Mayrks) has an insatiable appetite for winning races. As the son of a prosperous Brussels grocer, Eddy says he races out of love for the sport rather than money. A millionaire at the tender age of 27, this great athlete can well afford to make such statements. In 1972, his cycling skills were netting him $400,000 a year. In a 1970 poll taken by the Spanish magazine, *El Mundo*, he was voted the second most admired figure in the world, behind Ethel Kennedy, and in the United States where cycling is a relatively obscure sport, Eddy was being compared to such great athletes as Muhammad Ali.

At the age of 19, Merckx won the world amateur championship at Sallanches, France. One year later he turned professional and, in 1966, sprinted to victory in his first major event, the Milan-to-San Remo race. The following year the 5-foot-11-inch 165-pound cyclist captured the world professional championship. For the next several years "Cannibal Eddy" snapped up victories in every major race on the continent. In 1969, he blazed across the finish line in first place in the Tour de France, becoming the first Belgian in 30 years to accomplish that feat. As he was driven through the streets of Belgium to a victory celebration, thousands of his countrymen lined the route to honor their national hero.

Eddy is somewhat of an enigma to journalists. With his olive skin and coarse black hair, he appears to be more Latin than Flemish. His personality is two-fold, changing with his surroundings. On his bike he is cold, calculating, and quiet, but in his home near Brussels he is amiable, talkative, and extroverted.

As a child Merckx dreamed of being a champion cyclist, but when he voiced his ambitions as a teenager, his mother tried to discourage him. Eventually she relented and allowed him to drop out of school to race in addition to delivering groceries for his father.

Merckx has always given his best at whatever he attempted, whether it was road racing, exhibition basketball, or competing in a beer-drinking contest with fellow cyclist Jacques Anquetil. Within a few years of leaving school, he had captured the title, "World Professional Champion," and earned the right to wear the world champion's shirt. This shirt bears the label, MOLTEN 1, in addition to five stripes of blue, red, black, yellow, and green to signify all the countries of the world.

The hard-driving Merckx pedals as much as 21,000 miles during the 9-month racing season. He trains or races for 250 to 300 days each year, starting by riding 30 to 40 miles each day, and soon increasing the workouts to 90 to 125 miles daily. Eddy competes in about 120 races each year and has won more of them than anyone in history. He generally stays in peak condition with a heartbeat of 40 to 48 beats per minute. He competes in 60 to 80 exhibition races each year which are only 60 to 100 miles in length. They sometimes are only 2 hours long, and yet, he can earn as much as $4,000 in each one.

"Cannibal Eddy" leads the pack over the tooth-rattling cobblestones of Valenciennes in northern France to win the yellow jersey for the sixth leg of the 1970 Tour de France. He continued on to win the race which eventually netted him $375,000 from endorsements and other prizes.

Merckx takes great care of his equipment, checking with his mechanics over and over again before a race. He "cures" his tires for 3 years in his basement, and he uses bicycles of varying weights in his races. For sprints Eddy prefers an 18½-pound 10-speed bike, but in mountains he insists on the more stable, faster 22-pound 12-speed. In a Tour he usually requires three bicycles, although in the 1968 Tour d'Italie, he used twelve!

Unlike most racers Merckx does not use a coach and apparently does not need one, for he seems to have no real weaknesses. Eddy is not the fastest sprinter in the world, but his style is very powerful. He is not the best climber in the mountain stages, but here, too, he is strong. In the downhill sections Eddy is outstanding and has been clocked at 50 miles per hour. His competitors let him set the pace early in the race, but eventually he pulls away and they never see him again.

He seems to have no need for riding with a pack as he showed in the 1969 Tour de France. In crossing three treacherous, steep summits in the Pyrenees, he rode solo for 70 or 80 kilometers (42 to 48 miles). When he crossed the finish line, no one else was even in sight.

Racing is not smooth sailing all the way for Eddy as was seen in the 1970 Liège-Bastogne-Liège race. As he ascended a narrow dirt road near the finish, Eric de Vlaeminck of Belgium grabbed him by the shirt, disturbing his balance. Eric's brother, Roger, sprinted by and won the race. The judges did not see the incident and although Eddy was outraged, he did not file a complaint. He merely assumed he would get even next time. Eventually, helicopters were used to supervise the European races and put an end to such sabotage.

Merckx has also been plagued with accusations that he takes drugs during races. During the 1969 Tour d'Italie a urine specimen was demanded of Eddy since he was suspected of having taken tranquilizers. Although the drug was legal in Belgium, it was not in Italy. The specimen proved to be positive, but Merckx claimed it was not his. Eventually, the charges were dropped, but it was too late to rejoin the Tour. Later that year Eddy insisted that officials test him after each day's ride in the Tour de France.

When Eddy entered the 1970 Tour de France, his appetite for victory was keen. The French racers, on the other hand, appeared soft and unprepared, perhaps due to the demands of the continuous promotional deals which had come to dominate the sport. Merckx was again ready to prove his superiority during the brutal climbs through the Alps and the Pyrenees as well as in the death-defying downhill runs and full-tilt sprints over the vast plains. He was ready to put to rest the time-honored theories of strategy and pace upon which road racing had been founded.

At the start of the 120-mile stage from Lake Geneva across the Alps to Grenoble, 20 cyclists managed to keep Merckx in sight. When they reached the base of the first mountain, however, Eddy pulled away, leaving them far behind. As he crossed over the fourth summit at an altitude of 4,200 feet, he was totally alone. Plunging down the far side, he reached a speed of 50 miles per hour and, as if to show that he was totally in control, he casually pulled out a wrench and adjusted his seat. Merckx easily captured first place and gave the $100,000 first prize to his teammates and to charity. He eventually collected $375,000 from endorsements and other prizes.

After this victory he was ranked above Italy's Fausto Coppi and France's Jacques Anquetil, winner of four Tours from 1961 to 1964. It became a widespread belief that Eddy was going to win every Tour through 1975. In 1971, the Belgian raced in 120 events and won 53 of them including the Tour de France.

Although Merckx is generally in excellent condition, occasionally he suffers from severe cramps, apparently when he has not trained enough. In the 1971 Liège-Bastogne-Liège race, Eddy's stomach cramps almost became an insurmountable handicap. He was in pain for

161

"My job is winning races . . . It is not my fault if the competition is not what it should be."

3 days. On the final hill he held a 4-minute lead, but suddenly was afflicted by agonizing cramps. With barely 2 kilometers (1.2 miles) to go, Georges Pinton of Antwerp pulled alongside, and a brutal neck-and-neck sprint ensued. Suddenly, as they approached the track, Merckx's cramps vanished, allowing him to pull in front and win by a few feet.

The 1972 Tour de France was so disastrous that it became known as the Tour of the Crippled and Lame. On July 2, 1972, a total of 139 anxious, professional cyclists lined up in Angers for the start of the race. Three weeks later only 88 weary, beaten men pedaled across the finish in Paris. The 2,400-mile route laid

out for that year's race was murderous. More than half of the 20 brutal stages were in the mountains, and some had not been used in this event for nearly 10 years.

Merckx complained that the route was purposely favoring Spain's Luis Ocaña since he excelled in the mountains. It contained only three timed individual sprints, which were Merckx's strong point. In addition to the difficult layout of the race, the weather was anything but co-operative. The athletes were forced to suffer through drenching downpours which caused deadly mudslides, and on their exhausting ascents, they risked sunstroke and heat prostration.

Roger Pingeon, the winner of the 1967 Tour and the captain of the Peugeot-B.P.-Michelin team, admitted that he was literally afraid to go on. Apparently, he had almost gone out of control several times descending a mountain due to the rain and mud.

The dramatic battle between Merckx and Ocaña that reporters and fans had anticipated never materialized. Although the Spaniard was thought to be Merckx's stiffest competition, Ocaña had a history of serious problems in previous years. In 1969 and 1971 he had fallen during races, in 1970 he was plagued with hemorrhoids, and in 1972 bronchitis was his greatest foe. During the 1972 Tour, he collapsed in mid-race. Apparently, he had not raced enough that year and was inadequately prepared for the Tour.

Merckx's second greatest competitor in that race was a 25-year-old cyclist named Guimard. Merckx had been beaten by this superstar at least twice and was well aware of his incredible speed over mountains and flats alike. Normally, the battle would have been between Ocaña and Guimard, but Merckx's rapid pace broke the spirits of both of them. Ocaña dropped out of the race in the 14th lap.

Guimard looked strong and held first or second place for two thirds of the Tour. His knee, however, began giving him trouble, and by the 12th lap it was severely inflamed. The determined racer had a novocaine injection in his knee and attempted to finish the race for his team's sake. He miraculously won four laps and maintained his position in the front of the pack, but suddenly 8 miles into the 18th lap, he collapsed. Merckx had been merely 8 minutes ahead of him at the time. In spite of his being unable to complete the Tour, Guimard was appointed captain of the team the following year and collected a great deal of money from endorsements.

With Guimard out of the race, Eddy was now pursued by 36-year-old Raymond Poulidor who held a position 10 minutes behind Merckx but only 4 seconds in front of the Italian, Felice Gimondi. During the final three laps Poulidor fought gallantly to maintain his edge on Gimondi, but on the last lap he lived up to his image of being France's favorite loser, and fell behind him. Although he had raced since 1957, and always done extremely well, Poulidor had never once worn the *maillot jaune* for even a day. In 1972, he had respectfully stayed behind his faltering teammate, Guimard, rather than pass him even though he himself appeared strong throughout the race.

Eddy Merckx, meanwhile, was concentrating on winning, having taken the lead during the 8th lap and having held onto it securely. His victory was so certain that reporters and spectators grew bored. At the end of the 8th lap Merckx led by 2 minutes 33 seconds. He stretched the lead to 5 minutes 13 seconds by the end of 13 laps, and during the last stage from Versailles to Paris Eddy was separated from his competitors by 10 minutes. After winning all of the sprints, placing second in the mountain stages, and winning three other awards, Merckx raced across the finish with a smile on his face a full 10 minutes 41 seconds in front of Gimondi.

Rather than praising Merckx for his outstanding talents, the French press merely sulked, whining that Eddy had taken the suspense out of cycling and ruined it as a spectator sport. Apparently, some of the cyclists in the Tour were bad sports as well, for they were angered that he did not adhere to their unwritten rules. These were that normally a champion allows others to win some of the earlier prizes and that each athlete leads briefly as the race passes through his home town. However, in each race he entered Merckx sprinted into the lead shortly after the start and maintained a fast pace thereafter. Louison Bobet, three-time winner of the Tour de France, complained that Eddy was too professional and was only concerned with cycling, but as a public figure he owed something to his audience.

In answer to these complaints, Merckx coldly

Merckx leads Bernard Thevenet and Regis Ovion, both of France, in the last lap of the Tour de France as they pass the Arc de Triomphe on the Champs Elysées in Paris on July 20, 1975. Eddy is a famous superstar, his face being as familiar to Europeans as a movie star's or a king's.

replied, "My job is winning races . . . It is not my fault if the competition is not what it should be." Some have suggested caustically that Eddy should be handicapped by having his medicine cabinet locked or having him carry a 30-pound pack while he races.

In all likelihood it is Merckx's dedication, love for the sport, and ceaseless training— rather than merely drugs—which have made him a world champion. His popularity through-out Europe was shown in a cartoon placed in a Belgian newspaper. In it King Baudouin was reverently extending his hand to Eddy Merckx. An onlooker turned to his companion and asked, "Hey, who's that fellow shaking hands with Eddy?"

Eddy Merckx is to cycling what Brazil's Pelé has been to soccer. Even France's Jacques Anquetil admits that Merckx is "unbelievable."

38. Tour of the Sierra

It was an afternoon like any other with cars and pedestrians bustling along the main street in front of the Nevada state legislature building in Carson City. No one seemed to realize that this congested spot was the third stage finish for the 475-mile-long 1974 Tahoe-Donner Tour of the Sierra. A frantic Tour official fruitlessly attempted to shout over the city noise that a pack of cyclists would be blazing into town any minute at speeds of 30 miles per hour or more and, having covered 108.5 miles that day and climbed over 5,000 feet of steep mountain roads, they would be in no shape for dodging cars or stray dogs, nor for observing stop lights.

Fortunately, at the last minute a policeman appeared on the scene and blocked traffic. He arrived in the nick of time, for soon afterward the whirr of tires and click of pedals filled the streets. Just when the officials thought all was well, an oblivious, well-dressed woman stepped out into the road directly in front of the pack. The cyclists abruptly jammed on their brakes, but there was not enough time to stop. Suddenly, a spectator leaped from the crowd and knocked her out of the way just as the first racer whizzed by.

The cyclist who narrowly escaped the collision and captured first place that day was Mike Neel. The lady's only comment was a cynical one, "The government's falling apart and here are all these damn bicycles." Road racing in the United States is a far cry from that of the Tour de France and other events throughout Europe and Mexico. In France,

roads are closed to all automobile traffic, and huge crowds line the 3,000-mile route respectfully to applaud the athletes and catch a fleeting glimpse of their heroes. Villages and cities bid for the honor of having the Tour pass through their streets, while American communities rebel.

The 1974 Tour of the Sierra was the second longest bicycle race in the U.S. It was made up of a motley assortment of 80 young and old athletes, long-hairs and short-hairs, scientists and the unemployed, and one man who "striped parking lots" for a living. The unusual race consisted of 8 stages: a team time trial, five road races, a race over a short, closed course, and an individual time trial. The event took 7 days to complete, and 65 athletes finished all of the stages.

In Europe, athletes are trained by competent, qualified organizations that teach them racing strategy and team tactics. They learn to travel in packs, taking turns setting the pace and providing windbreaks for teammates behind them. They are taught how to jockey for better positions and when to pull away from the pack and sprint.

In the United States, where racers have little if any formal training, packs are loose, and racers are individualists. They must be in top condition, however, to race at full speed for 5 or more hours each day for 7 days or more. Unlike Belgium's Eddy Merckx, who makes $625,000 a year from road races, and other European cyclists who collect $100,000 annually, Americans must pay their own expenses and compete merely for tires, bike pumps, and kisses. Rick ("Captain America") Hammen, who was formerly a theoretical chemist, eventually opted for unemployment so that he could race full time in America.

The sport has grown at a fast pace in recent years, for in 1962 only 60 cyclists were registered in northern California while in 1974 there were over a thousand. With the growth of the sport has come an increase in injuries and tragedies. Only one road racer was killed in the U.S. between 1920 and 1974, but in 1974 alone three racers died as a result of accidents, even though wearing helmets.

Better organization and a greater respect for cyclists are required in the U.S. In the 1974 Tour of the Sierra, Dan Nall from Santa Cruz was hit by a truck. Another vulnerable racer, Jack Janelle of Littleton, California, was trapped between two cattle trucks and eventually forced off the road and down a 30-foot cliff. Surprisingly enough, both of these determined racers finished the event.

On the lighter side, the second oldest man in the Tour, 41-year-old Nick Farac of San Francisco, finished strong in the tough, week-long event and was awarded a prize of a free session at Nevada's legal Moonlight Ranch sporting house.

The 105-mile second stage of the 1974 Tour of the Sierra was a fiasco from the start. The 80 cyclists and their retinue of trainers, officials, managers, et al, backed up cars and trailer trucks on the highway for miles. The California Highway Patrol, lights flashing and sirens wailing, screamed alongside the athletes, nearly hitting them in the confusion. The patrolmen bellowed that the riders would have to pedal single file on the far right-hand edge of the highway.

In Sierraville matters grew from bad to unbelievable as officer Dean Rupp, a burly, authoritative member of the California Highway Patrol, brought the race to a standstill for 45 minutes. He pulled out the State Vehicle Code and patiently showed the race officials where it said, "Bicycle riders must ride as close to the right-hand curb as possible." The policeman was totally unfamiliar with bicycle racing tactics, such as riding in packs and jockeying for position, and could not understand why they rode bunched together. Finally, after lengthy explanations the patrolman approved, and the next time the cyclists whizzed through his territory, he merely yelled, "Hello, peoples."

The race continued on around scenic Lake Tahoe, through the main streets of Reno and Truckee, and along Highway 49, the gold rush route of 1849. Much of the race passed through ponderosa pines, mesquite bushes, and sagebrush. The beauty of the Sierras and the sheer thrill of competition was what this race was all about. Road racing in America provides few rewards other than this, and it is never likely to be converted into big-money competition, as in Europe.

U.S. cyclists seem to appreciate the style and flavor of local road races, but some such as Mike Neel from Berkeley, the winner of the 1974 Tour of the Sierra, feel differently. As a 22-year-old semi-professional, Neel would rather be hired by a foreign team where in addition to making money from the sport, he would no longer have to brake for oblivious little old ladies.

39. The First North American Bicycle Championship

It was the race that outshone the Tour de France in all aspects except distance. The first North American Bicycle Championship was conceived by a group of men from Colorado who were convinced that America's youths were soft. A course was needed that would be tougher than the annual 41 laps around Somerville, New Jersey, so Bert Bidwell, Bernie ("Big Wheel") Witkin, and the Aspen Chamber of Commerce worked on a plan.

They came up with a brutal endurance test— a course 190 miles long which crossed the Continental Divide twice and reached some of the highest peaks in North America. The race would start in Aspen, Colorado, pass through Glenwood Springs and Leadville, and return to Aspen. The cyclists would have to pedal over two steep mountain passes and part of a third, including treacherous Independence Pass which promised snow or sleet even in September.

The race was originally scheduled for July, 1965, but at the last minute the Amateur Bicycle League had it postponed until mid-September. This poor management decision cut the expected field of entrants from 70 to 16 since many of the racers were students.

Since the descent from the summit was dangerous too and rocky, Jim Crist, a Denver teacher and ski patrolman, planned to exchange his fragile racing bike at this point for an old, heavy Schwinn with thick tires for speed and stability.

On the first stage of the first day of the punishing 2-day event the cyclists were to sprint 41 miles from Aspen to Glenwood Springs. From there they were to proceed in the second stage northeast into the 2,500-foot-deep Glenwood Canyon, 60 miles on past Gypsum, up Battle Mountain, through the Tennessee Pass, into the Arkansas Valley, and on to Leadville. Leadville at 10,152 feet is the highest incorporated city in North America.

The second day's ride was no easier. In fact, in that single day the athletes were to ride from Leadville to Aspen by crossing four 14,000-foot peaks and several dozen 13,000-foot ones. This climb is so steep that gold miners once used 20-mule teams to haul their wagons over the mountain range. They then lowered them down using ropes.

The athletes arrived early Saturday morning for the start from Paepcke Park in Aspen. Many carried raw meat, fruit, and dextrose tablets as fuel for the exhausting race. At 10 a.m. they crossed the starting line and sprinted through the center of town, reaching speeds of 45 miles per hour.

The roads were slick from the previous night's rainstorm when the cyclists approached their first obstacle, the Rio Grande railroad crossing. The first victim was Dick Oldakowski who hit the rails at an angle and flipped over backward. Four more riders directly behind crashed into him. Only 8 men passed this point unhurt. By the time their trainers replaced their bikes and

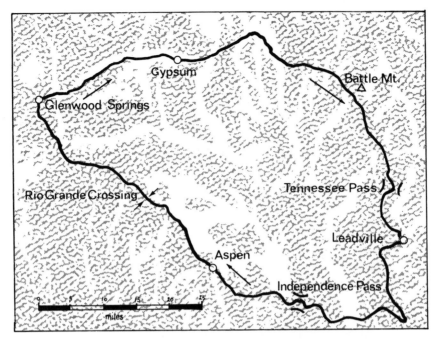

Route of the North American Bicycle Championship.

applied bandages, their competitors had an enormous lead. The original plan had been to stay in a pack and sprint near the end of each stage to compete for bonus prizes.

When the cyclists reached Carbondale, they hit roads made of gravel and red mud. By the time they completed the first of the three stages, the men were red from head to foot. Steve Hammond covered the 41-mile first stage in 1 hour 23 minutes 52 seconds, putting him in first place. As a bonus, officials subtracted a minute from his time.

Dick Oldakowski, after seriously injuring himself at the railroad crossing, managed to complete the first stage. When he sprinted over the finish, however, he fell from his bike in great pain. He struggled back onto his feet, methodically brushed himself off, cleaned his bike, and wearily hitched a ride back to Aspen. Gary Wilson was another victim of the railroad crossing fiasco, but when the doctors ordered him from the race, he refused to quit.

After a brief, 15-minute rest, the 14 remain-ing cyclists mounted their bikes and left Glenwood Springs with a police escort. The first stage had been brutal, and yet, this was easy compared to what was to come. The oldest entrant in the race, 60-year-old Lawrence Gordon, caught up to the pack just as they took off on the second stage.

The race started to take its toll between the end of Glenwood Canyon and Gypsum for two more riders quit and a third slacked off on his pace, dropping back from the pack. As the determined group headed on toward Eagle, they hit a powerful headwind which forced them into riding single file. Later, while battling fierce crosswinds, they stretched themselves diagonally across the road. After struggling on in this manner for an hour and a half, they finally reached Eagle but were stopped by a patrolman for riding more than two abreast. The delay stiffened up their exhausted muscles so badly that Steve Hammond was forced to pedal with only one leg.

In another 3 miles Bill Scott quit the race.

A little further on, Hammond, although holding the lead in spite of his bad leg, also dropped out. Kal Halasi took over the lead, but 52 miles remained between him and victory. Jim Crist was only 16 seconds behind him, and Stu Pray only 31 seconds back.

As the Continental Divide loomed before them, Halasi reduced his speed, and Crist took over the elapsed time lead, followed by Pray and Bob Weedin. As they approached the steep grade up Battle Mountain, the athletes sprinted to get a strong start. Immediately, the racers, including Crist, slowed down one by one, except for Pray and John Marshall.

After the exhausting 5-mile climb, these two front runners, still holding the lead, began coasting down the far side at speeds of 60 miles per hour or more. Although this was treacherous, they needed the speed as they began the next climb to the 10,424-foot-high Tennessee Pass. Pray suffered cramps during this 15-mile stretch, but managed to stay with his opponent and was only 0.9 of a second behind Marshall as they sprinted into Leadville and across the finish for that stage. Crist joined them only 4 minutes later.

There was much local interest in this race as citizens followed the events on their radios, and police escorted each athlete through guarded intersections and across the finish. The mayor acted as bartender at a party held afterwards in honor of the racers, and John Marshall was awarded a gold watch. There was a rumor circulating that Gary Wilson had broken his arm, but had pedaled the last 115 miles anyway. Lawrence Gordon, completing the run an hour and a half after the leaders, was greeted by cheers.

After a raucous dinner and a good night's sleep, the 10 remaining cyclists rode down California Gulch in a sleet storm and headed for the finish line in Aspen, 59 miles away. After breezing through Arkansas Valley at 40 m.p.h., they spotted a welcome sign reading INDEPENDENCE PASS OPEN. After slipping into low gear, the athletes passed Twin Lakes and approached Perry Mountain. In 1962, a silent avalanche on this mountain had engulfed three houses and taken six lives while the neighbors, only 50 yards away, heard nothing.

At 10,300 feet the altitude took its toll on Halasi, Wally Dziak, and Tom Meyer. Seven cyclists riding close together circled around Star Mountain and suddenly spotted the steep switchbacks they were to ascend. Their trainers readied oxygen tanks and extra tires as the men reached the gravel road. Patrick Dennis stopped to change tires, while Pray and Marshall sprinted on with Crist only 100 feet behind them. Marshall steadily pulled away from Pray until by the third switchback, he was out of view. He passed the summit a full 2 minutes ahead of his opponents and much faster than prior predictions.

As he started the difficult descent over the slippery gravel road, Marshall closed his brakes slightly and began skidding through the dangerous turns at 30 to 35 miles per hour. Suddenly, a tire blew near the ghost town of Independence. Bidwell, one of the sponsors, immediately turned his jeep around and headed back to search for a spare tire. When he returned, Marshall was nowhere in sight. A sympathetic spectator in a Volkswagen had given the helpless cyclist his $79 bike with about 7 pounds of air in the tires. It was a comic sight, however, for Marshall could not reach the pedals. He took off anyway, while attempting to lower the seat with a wrench.

Meanwhile Bidwell radioed the finish line that the cyclists would be arriving much sooner than expected. As it turned out, Marshall reached the finish of the 2-day ordeal before most of the spectators had arrived. Pray was barely 48 seconds back, and Crist finished third. The overall, elapsed time-finish revealed that Marshall won the 190-mile race in 9 hours 25 minutes 22 seconds, only 17 seconds in front of second place.

Independence Pass took a severe toll on the other racers, in particular Weedin. He broke a chain, flattened a tire, lost his rear brakes, crushed a wheel, flattened four more tires, got stranded with no help in sight, rode on his flat tire, and ruined another wheel. In all the cyclists used up 34 tires, 9 wheels, 12 chains, numerous sprockets, headsets, freewheels, cranks, brakes, pedals, and feeder bottles. On the injury list were four athletes with severely damaged arms and legs.

Bicycle road racers are generally a hardy bunch, being used to ducking beer cans and rotten eggs thrown from passing cars, in addition to surviving torturous mountain climbs and brutal bone-breaking falls. After the first North American Bicycle Championship, however, Jim Crist remarked that racing was exciting enough without adding life-threatening conditions.

40. An American in Paris: Creig Hoyt and the Paris-Brest-Paris Race

The 750-mile race from Paris to oceanside Brest and back again is one of the most demanding cycling events in the world and yet has thrived since its inception in 1895. In 1975, it provided the setting for one of the most exciting sports stories of the year.

Although most of the competitors that year were European amateur and professional cyclists, a small group of adventurous and determined Americans were also entered. Among them was a 33-year-old ophthalmologist from the University of California Hospital who was attempting to become the first cyclist from the U.S. to complete the punishing race and the first American to cycle 750 miles in less than 90 hours.

The first time Creig Hoyt attempted this was in 1971, but that year his hopes were dashed when his bicycle was stolen from the Frankfurt Airport. It mysteriously reappeared a month later after the race was over. For the next 4 years Creig spent all of his spare time, outside of his busy medical practice, training for the race. He managed to put in 800 miles each week on his bike in addition to 50 or 60 miles of running. He even had a friend build a custom-made lightweight bicycle made of graphite.

He persistently badgered the airlines to assure him that his new bike would be well treated, but when he changed planes in Los Angeles to take off for Paris, he could not believe his ears. The airport personnel told him that his bike had been lost on the flight from San Francisco. Amid promises of its safe return, Hoyt reluctantly boarded the plane and left for France. Miraculously, it turned up soon after, and was shipped to Paris.

Four other Americans met with Creig in the Latin Quarter of Paris to devise a game plan. Hoyt's friend, Dr. Herman Falsetti, a cardiologist from the University of Iowa Hospital, was there, having talked with Creig over the summer about racing with him. An 18-year-old girl, Cathy Hillan, from Santa Clara, California, was also present but was worried about a serious fall she had taken while training in Europe that summer.

Another woman anxiously awaiting the start was a touring cyclist from Chicago named Maggie Tekstar. She had faithfully pedaled over 300 miles each week that summer and in August had flown to France to cycle-tour the entire route the race would follow. During the pre-race strategy sessions her knowledge of the course was a valuable asset. The fifth American racer was James Konski, a civil engineer from Syracuse, New York. He knew he could not maintain the fast pace the others planned but was going to attempt to complete the event in 90 hours.

The group pored over detailed maps as

Maggie pointed out the route the race was to follow. Most of it was along highways, but there were also 100 miles or more of confusing back roads. When Creig and the others arrived at the starting point, they were dumbfounded at the reception they got. As they received their numbers, a jovial, enthusiastic official, Monsieur Lepertel, announced their presence over the loudspeaker. Although there were over 700 cyclists from all over the Continent, the Americans were treated like royalty. Soon, however, they began to feel out of place since the European cyclists had sponsors, mechanics, and trucks while all they had were a few friends. When the French press, including television newsmen, began interviewing them, the Americans became even more nervous.

Suddenly, their carefully thought-out plans and strategy were disrupted when they learned that the women would start 15 minutes before the men. Falsetti and Hoyt had intended to stay with the two girls, but now they would be on their own. As the race started, there were so many competitors that they formed packs of 20 and crossed the starting line in brief intervals. Creig, Herman, and Jim sprinted through the mass of cyclists and soon were chasing the lead pack.

The men were surprised to spot Maggie soon afterward, but she had fallen badly near the start and was doing poorly. At this point Jim slowed down, and the American team split up. Creig and Herman stayed together, sprinted past Cathy, and headed for the lead group of about 200 cyclists. The two Americans breezed through the first hundred miles arriving at the first check point in $4\frac{1}{2}$ hours.

At dusk Hoyt encountered a serious problem. His light was not nearly so powerful as the huge flashlights the French racers had attached to their bikes. They could see 75 yards ahead, while he could only see a few feet, so he decided to fall in behind them. This worked for a while, but soon a fog bank rolled in, obscuring everything from view. Barely able to see 20 feet in front of him, Hoyt desperately tried to chase

the French lights anyway. Throughout the night as he flew down steep grades, he found himself slowing for curves only when he heard the screech of bicycle brakes ahead of him.

As dawn lit the skies, Creig was astounded to see French men and women lining the route, cheering all who passed by. Arriving at the fourth checkpoint in Rennes on the second day, Hoyt learned that he had covered 225 miles in less than 14 hours. Fatigue and depression were becoming overwhelming, however, and he sat down to rest.

Suddenly, he thought he was hallucinating when he saw a French cyclist sitting on the grass across from him eating a hearty meal of spaghetti, bread, and even wine. Hoyt was on the verge of quitting, while this man was leisurely enjoying a picnic!

Creig, both humiliated and inspired, jumped back on his bike and headed for Brest. The final 100 miles to the ocean were torturous since they consisted of endless rolling hills. Hoyt fought uphill through the "Walls of Brest"—25-mile-an-hour headwinds whipping in from the English Channel.

Although Hoyt and Falsetti had originally planned to race straight through without stopping, Creig learned on the second day that no one except the lead group attempts this. After he had been on his bike for 24 hours, Hoyt decided to stop and sleep for 6 hours in Brest. As he approached the city, he could not believe his eyes. The lead racers, bunched together, were heading back to Paris and were not only sprinting at full speed, but looked fresh and rejuvenated. They had covered 400 miles in 24 hours but looked as if they were just starting the event.

In Brest, spectators and racers alike were surprised at the early arrival of the Americans. Unfortunately, the hotels were filled, but four of them managed to crowd into the one available single room. In the morning they felt great, but the break had taken 11 hours. Hoyt and Falsetti were now in 220th place. They sprinted to the next checkpoint and climbed in the standings. Throughout the afternoon they munched on sweets and mineral water and by nightfall were in 150th place. Suddenly, Herman began hallucinating, and Hoyt loyally took him to a hotel.

When he returned to the race, Creig joined a pack of astonished Frenchmen who could not believe how well he was doing. They maintained a brisk pace of 20 miles per hour and caught up to a British cyclist, Dr. Clifford Graves. He wisely warned them that the roads ahead were tricky so they should be careful not to get lost. The group sprinted over the flat farmlands, and when they arrived at the next checkpoint, there were only 70 cyclists ahead of them.

Three of them stopped to refresh themselves, but Hoyt frantically pushed on. There were only 100 miles to go, but the American was exhausted and entirely alone. He blindly raced up and down hills barely aware of where he was. He looked behind him and spotted a French support car. Then his heart sank as he saw a pack of cyclists catching up to him. Pumping his aching legs as fast as possible, he kept them from passing him. Suddenly they disappeared as quickly as they had appeared, and Creig realized he was hallucinating!

He was horrified to see cars in front of him, but then realized that they were only sheep. The next moment, he found himself lying on the ground looking at his bike and a pedal that had broken off. He had crashed. With only 30 miles remaining he could not quit, so he ran his bike up hills and coasted down them. He tried pedaling with just his left leg, but soon he was in pain and exhausted.

Miraculously, Phil Bartel, his friend and mechanic appeared over a hill and saw Creig signaling him. Soon, with his pedal replaced, Hoyt was back in the race, having lost only a few positions during the delay. Disaster struck once more, however, as he approached the final hill. He again found himself on the ground, this time with the derailleur—the gear-mechanism—broken and twisted among the spokes. His bicycle was now a total loss and only 12 miles separated him from the finish in Paris. To make matters more frustrating, he was now in first or second place, because everyone else was fighting disaster too. Spent, nearly hysterical, and in tears, Hoyt merely sat by the road, screaming for Phil, who was by now awaiting him at the finish line.

At this moment, a farmer approached in his car and sympathetically asked what had happened. When Hoyt explained, the man drove ahead in search of Phil. Unable to find him, the farmer returned and offered Creig his son's tiny bike with 20-inch wheels, balloon tires, and a bell which rang incessantly. Creig was overjoyed and quickly pedaled off, not seeming to mind that he had to stand to keep his knees from hitting the handlebars.

Finally, the finish line was in sight and he was surrounded by a crowd of awe-struck spectators who were astounded that an American was even finishing the race. As he crossed over on the child's bike, the tiny bell's clatter was drowned out by cheers. Although Creig had lost 30 to 35 positions due to his final breakdown, he was ecstatic that he had finished in under 66 hours. Herman Falsetti arrived after 74 hours, and Cathy Hillan after 83 hours. Jim Konski was pedaling strongly and steadily but had to quit 100 miles outside of Paris after the 90-hour time limit had run out.

Maggie Tekstar was not so fortunate as her teammates. Having hit her head in her fall, she had been hospitalized outside of Paris. The brutal race had reaped its toll from several others as well. Three French cyclists were hit by a truck which killed two of them.

Creig Hoyt swore he would never enter the race again, but after receiving flowers and a trophy the next day for being the first Americans ever to finish the Paris-Brest-Paris Race, both he and Herman knew they would probably be back.

Index

Fl